RENEWING
THE VISION

Reformed Faith
for the 21st Century

Cynthia M. Campbell, editor

Geneva Press
Louisville, Kentucky

© 2000 Geneva Press

Scripture quotations from the New Revised Standard Version of the Bible are copyright © 1989 by the Division of Christian Education of the National Council of the Churches of Christ in the U.S.A. and are used by permission.

Acknowledgments will be found on page xiii.

Book design by Sharon Adams
Cover design by Dean Nicklas

First edition

Published by Geneva Press
Louisville, Kentucky

This book is printed on acid-free paper that meets the American National Standards Institute Z39.48 standard. ∞

PRINTED IN THE UNITED STATES OF AMERICA

00 01 02 03 04 05 06 07 08 09 — 10 9 8 7 6 5 4 3 2 1

Library of Congress Cataloging-in-Publication Data

A catalog record for this book is available from the Library of Congress.
ISBN 0-664-50124-9

Contents

Introduction

Theology Matters

In 1994 the General Assembly of the Presbyterian Church (U.S.A.) responded to a complex and potentially deeply divisive controversy by issuing a statement that reminded the church that, among other things, "theology matters." Amid decisions about church governance and administrative oversight, at the heart of controversies over ordination and worship, beneath debates about leadership and accountability, regardless of the specific topics, it is our theology that matters.

This is a distinctively "Reformed" claim: that the core of disputes in the church can, and indeed *should*, be traced back to what we believe about God. John Calvin, from whom Presbyterian or Reformed Christians trace our intellectual heritage, built his theological house on the foundation of the sovereignty (or, one might say, the preeminence) of God. This is far from an abstract claim. It is not "God-in-general," a Higher Power or Supreme Being, whose centrality Calvin proclaimed. Rather, it is the God who made covenant with humanity through Israel, who is seen most clearly in the love and justice of Jesus Christ, whose sovereign power is known through the triumph of divine grace, what Hendrikus Berkhof called "holy love."

For Reformed Christians, theology matters, and what matters most in theology is God. In practical terms, this means that the issues that confront us in both church and world eventually turn on who we understand God to be and how we see ourselves and others in relation to God. The "Preliminary Principles" of the *Book of Order*, which trace their origin to the organizing of Presbyterianism in America, state that "truth is in order to

goodness; and the great touchstone of truth, its tendency to promote holiness, according to our Savior's rule, 'By their fruits ye
shall know them.' . . . [W]e are persuaded that there is an inseparable connection between faith and practice, truth and duty"
(G-1.0304).

Theological conviction and everyday life in both church and
world are intimately connected. We attempt to know God and
our relationship with God in order to know how to live with God
and neighbor. We examine actions, decisions, programs, and
statements and ask what vision of God stands behind them. We
look at the consequences of our words and deeds and seek to discern which paths lead toward the God revealed in Jesus Christ.

Beyond this conviction of the preeminence or centrality of
God, there has never been complete agreement about what the
Book of Order calls the "essential tenets" of Reformed faith.
Most recent attempts to specify "the essentials" (beyond the
statement found in the constitution at G-2.0500) have been
rejected. In part, this is because the Reformed tradition has
always allowed a diversity of specific expression. It is also a
recognition that Reformed theology is a *way* of reflecting on
Christian faith and practice as much as it is a set of specific doctrines or unique ideas.

Several principles guide this Reformed way of thinking about
Christian faith. First, Reformed theological reflection is grounded on the witness of scripture. When Reformed folk say that
"theology matters," they mean that the Bible matters—the Bible
as story of God and God's people, as record of faith, as source of
values, as witness to the person and power of Jesus Christ. The
Bible is the place Reformed Christians begin and to which we
return in the journey of discernment.

Second, the Bible is not the Word of God in some abstract or
absolute sense. The Bible is God's Word to us today, as the Holy
Spirit enables us to read and hear and comprehend what is contained within it. Thus, interpretation of scripture depends on
God's lively presence with us and on our presence to and with
one another. Reformed Christians have always argued that we
come to apprehend the Word of God through speaking and listening, studying and sharing; through conversation and even

debate, under the guidance of the Spirit. Knowing the Bible as God's Word depends both on God and on our presence with one another in the community of faith.

Third, Reformed Christians believe that theology that matters grows up out of the context in which believers find themselves. We live now, at the turn of the twenty-first century, not in the first or sixteenth or nineteenth century. We live here, in North America, specifically in the United States, not in Europe or Africa or Latin America. We are confronted by the issues of our day and time and place, some of which are deeply rooted in the past and some of which are challenges unique to this age. Reformed Christians have taken seriously the task of writing confessions of faith, catechisms, and theological affirmations because we believe that, just as the Word became flesh in a particular person in a particular time and place, so faith takes form and is formed by the specific places in which believers find themselves. This does not mean that words from other times and places are not relevant for today. It does mean that we cannot simply rely on those who have gone before to do all of our theological reflection for us; rather, we must be actively engaged in this process for ourselves.

A fourth conviction, which follows from the last, is that we will never complete the task of theological reflection; we will never write an infallible theological document; we will never comprehend, let alone be able to express, all of who God is and what we are to be and do in relationship to God. Theology matters, but it is an utterly human enterprise. As such, it will always be flawed and partial, always open to reform, renewal, and revision. Despite the strength of conviction with which many Reformed theologians have written, our tradition believes that theological reflection must be engaged in with humility toward God and charity toward one another.

Theological Reflection in Context

Controversy about Christian belief and practice is nothing new to the life of the Presbyterian Church, as several of the essays in this book describe. One of the current debates in this as in many American denominations is over the status of gay and lesbian members. Specifically for Presbyterians, the question is whether or not these members, if they are sexually active, are eligible for ordination and leadership in the life of the church.

The debate began in 1974 when the General Assembly was first asked whether a "self-avowed and practicing" homosexual person, duly called by a congregation, could be installed in office. The answer in 1978 by the United Presbyterian Church (U.S.A.) was a statement of "definitive guidance" that ordination and installation for such persons was inappropriate. While this statement was later termed an "authoritative interpretation," attempts both to overturn it and to make that language part of the constitution continued.

In 1996 the General Assembly proposed to the presbyteries that the *Book of Order* be amended in the following way:

> Those who are called to office in the church are to lead a life in obedience to Scripture and in conformity to the historic confessional standards of the church. Among these standards is the requirement to live either in fidelity within the covenant of marriage between a man and a woman (W-4.9001), or chastity in singleness. Persons refusing to repent of any self-acknowledged practice which the confessions call sin shall not be ordained and/or installed as deacons, elders, or ministers of the Word and Sacrament. (G-6.0106b)

At the next General Assembly, where the affirmative vote by the presbyteries on that language was reported and the amendment was placed in the constitution, another amendment was sent to the presbyteries that significantly modified the language by removing the reference to "chastity in singleness" and replaced it with language about integrity in all relationships of life.

Although that attempt to modify G-6.0106b was defeated by the presbyteries, debate on the issue, actions in various courts of the church to test the interpretation of the provision, and charges against specific individuals have continued. Out of this struggle, a group was formed that came to be called the Covenant Network of Presbyterians. While, initially, not all its members shared the same convictions with respect to the ordination of gay and lesbian persons, this group of pastors, teachers, officers, and members was convinced that G-6.0106b was flawed legislation, based on faulty theology.

In 1998 the Covenant Network committed itself to ongoing efforts in the Presbyterian Church to engage ordination and other church-dividing issues in a spirit of dialogue, in search of both renewal and unity. To that end, "A Call to Covenant Community" was adopted to provide a theological framework around which to gather and from which to enter discussions throughout the church. (See Appendix.) This book is a collection of essays and sermons designed to reflect on the key themes of that statement.

The statement, and thus this book, is divided into five themes. The first affirms that Jesus Christ is the center and ground of faith and practice, who invites us to join in his ministry of being and bringing good news.

The second theme focuses on the nature of the church called into being by the person and work of Jesus Christ. As Christ welcomed all—indeed, as he sought out and invited in those who were outside and estranged—so the church is envisioned as a community of hospitality.

The third theme stresses the mission of the church as it seeks to live out its calling to be "light to the nations," not from a position of privilege but as servant and partner with others who also seek justice, freedom, and peace.

The role of scripture and the ways in which the church wrestles with the task of interpretation form the fourth section. The essays and sermons herein reflect the convictions stated above concerning the role of the Spirit and of the community in hearing God's word for us today.

Finally, the statement affirms that those who would follow Christ must wrestle with the call to unity in Christ's name. This is especially difficult in the face of volatile ethical and social issues. But the call to seek unity amid the diversity that is one of God's gifts to us remains at the heart of Christian identity.

In the fall of 1998, the executive committee of the Covenant

Network decided to solicit essays and sermons that would reflect on the themes of "A Call to Covenant Community" and to offer them to the church as part of the ongoing project of dialogue and discernment. Jane Dempsey Douglass, Sheila Gustafson, Jack Rogers, and I formed the editorial committee. We are deeply grateful to all who responded so readily and creatively to make contributions to this volume. As general editor, I am particularly grateful to Sheila Gustafson, for overseeing the collection and editing of the sermons, and to Helen DeLeon, for bringing all the parts of the manuscript into a whole.

It is our hope that this collection will become a resource for those who want to engage in thoughtful reflection on the demands of the gospel in our particular context. The essays and sermons are offered not as "last words" on the issues before us but rather as occasions for reflection, as conversation starters, and as aids to dialogue. We have not produced a study guide to this volume, although one is available for "A Call to Covenant Community."

Harry Emerson Fosdick, although he never became a Presbyterian, was at the center of a bitter and difficult theological struggle in the Presbyterian Church in the early years of the twentieth century. His great hymn "God of Grace and God of Glory" has become one of the standards of Presbyterian worship. The prayer which is that hymn sums up the theme and the hope of this volume: "Grant us wisdom, grant us courage, for the living of these days!" We believe that God has called us to live and work, to think and act and pray, in these days, with these particular challenges. Our work here is an effort to speak the Word as we have heard it in these, our days.

Cynthia M. Campbell

Acknowledgments

Grateful acknowledgment is made to the following for permission to quote from copyrighted material.

From "Eat This Bread, Drink This Cup," *Music from Taizé: Responses, Litanies, Acclamations, Canons,* volume II. Copyright 1982, 1983, and 1984 Les Presses de Taizé (France). Used with permission of G.I.A. Publications, Inc., 7404 South Mason Avenue, Chicago, Illinois 60638 (U.S.A.).

From Brian Wren, "We Are Your People," copyright © 1975 by Hope Publishing Company, Carol Stream, IL 60188. All rights reserved. Used by permission of Hope Publishing Company.

From Megan McKenna and Tony Cowan, *Keepers of the Story* (Maryknoll, N.Y.: Orbis Books, 1997). Used by permission of Orbis Books.

From J. M. Coetzee, *Age of Iron* (New York: Random House, 1990). Used by permission of Random House, Inc.

Contributors

Joanna M. Adams
Pastor, Trinity Presbyterian Church
Atlanta, Georgia

Ellen L. Babinsky
Associate Professor of Church History
Austin Presbyterian Theological Seminary

Brian K. Blount
Associate Professor of New Testament
Princeton Theological Seminary

Robert Bohl
Pastor, The Village Church
Prairie Village, Kansas

John M. Buchanan
Pastor, Fourth Presbyterian Church
Chicago, Illinois

Cynthia M. Campbell
President
McCormick Theological Seminary

Robert A. Chesnut
Pastor, East Liberty Presbyterian Church
Pittsburgh, Pennsylvania

Jane Dempsey Douglass
Professor Emerita
Princeton Theological Seminary

Anna Carter Florence
Instructor in Preaching and Worship
Columbia Theological Seminary

Sheila C. Gustafson
Pastor, First Presbyterian Church
Santa Fe, New Mexico

Shirley C. Guthrie
Professor Emeritus
Columbia Theological Seminary

Karen Hernández-Granzen
Pastor, Westminster Presbyterian Church
Trenton, New Jersey

William H. Hopper, Jr.
Presbyterian minister, retired
Duarte, California

Linda C. Loving
Pastor, House of Hope Presbyterian Church
St. Paul, Minnesota

W. Eugene March
A. B. Rhodes Professor of Old Testament
   and Professor of Bible and Spirituality
Louisville Presbyterian Theological Seminary

Deborah F. Mullen
Assistant Professor of Ministry and Historical Studies
   and Dean of Master's Level Programs
McCormick Theological Seminary

Amy Plantinga Pauw
Henry P. Mobley Jr. Professor of Doctrinal Theology
Louisville Presbyterian Theological Seminary

Jack Rogers
Professor Emeritus
San Francisco Theological Seminary

Letty M. Russell
Professor of Theology
Yale Divinity School

Laird J. Stuart
Pastor, Calvary Presbyterian Church
San Francisco, California

Jon M. Walton
Pastor, Westminster Presbyterian Church
Wilmington, Delaware

PART 1

Believing
God's Good News

The Good News

Shirley C. Guthrie

All talk about believing and living by God's good news (and whether or not we actually do believe and live by it) is frivolous and divisive unless we have a clear and common understanding of what that good news is. In this essay I discuss some of its basic affirmations that seem to me to be most at stake—and most at risk—for authentic Christian faith and life in the church today.

The Good News about God

According to the writings of the New Testament, the good news is that with the coming of Jesus of Nazareth, ancient Israel's hope for the coming reign of God was being fulfilled. Jesus was not only one who proclaimed the dawning reign of God; in what he said and did, he himself *was* the reign of God breaking into the world. He was despised and rejected by both the political and the religious establishment (and, finally, by most of his own followers) and put to death by capital punishment. But he was not just a martyred teacher and example of a higher morality, a deeper truth about God, a more genuine spirituality, and a new vision of social justice, who left his followers to put into practice as best they could what they had learned

3

from him. God raised the crucified Jesus from the dead and made him living Lord who, by his Spirit, continues to be at work establishing the reign of God not only in the hearts of Christians and their community but also outside the Christian circle throughout the whole world. And he will continue his work until finally there is a whole new humanity in a whole new heaven and earth.

As the Reformed tradition has always insisted, therefore, authentic Christian faith is faith in the past, present, and future Word and work of the living triune God of the Bible. It is not faith in what *Christians* should and can say and do. What Christians affirm is not *their* faith in Christ but *God's* faithfulness in and through him, not *their* commitment to the cause of God in the world but *God's* commitment to it.

Christians are not people who believe that the integrity of the church and hope for the world depends on the acceptance and defense of any old or new doctrines *about* God. They are not people who (along with people of other faiths and many without any faith) are committed to the "ideals" of justice, freedom, love, and peace and to this or that liberal or conservative political agenda in order to "realize" these ideals and fix everything that is wrong with the world. They are not people who (along with many non-Christians) believe that a renewed commitment to "moral absolutes" and "family values" will solve all our personal and social problems. They are not people who place their hope in the renewal that can be achieved in this or that program of spiritual development.

Christians are people who believe in the living God who was present and at work long before they came along, is present and at work now, and will still be present and at work long after they are gone. They believe and hope in what their crucified and risen Lord by his Spirit can and will do in and for the church and world, with or without their help and cooperation. They are sure that God's reign will come and God's will *will* be done, despite the inadequate best they can do to make it happen or the worst they can do to prevent it from happening. The good news is that Christians are relieved of the terrible burden, arrogant pretension, and blasphemy of believing that *they* should or can be the instructors, lords, saviors, reconcilers, and renewers of the world. That job has already been taken.

We need not be afraid that such a God-centered faith means that we can sit back and "let God do it." On the contrary, when our faith is grounded in the good news about the living triune God, we discover that this God both requires and enables not less but far more demanding Christian discipleship and faithful witness than we have imagined.

God's Inclusive Love

The good news is that the God we come to know in the story of Jesus (as already in the story of ancient Israel) is a God who invites outsiders in, accepts the unacceptable, chooses the rejected, includes the excluded, and loves the unloved and unlovable—without any qualifications that must be met before they are eligible to be recipients of such love.

Jesus announced that he came to defend the cause of the poor against the rich and powerful who oppressed them. But he also invited into the company of his followers rich people such as the tax collector Matthew, who worked for a totalitarian foreign government and ran a lucrative business extracting from the poor more money than the government demanded of them. He said that his followers should love their enemies, but he invited into his inner circle a right-wing nationalistic freedom fighter, Simon the Zealot. He was a faithful Jew who worshiped and served the God of Israel, but he befriended and came to the aid of people of questionable religious faith with whom his fellow Jews would have nothing to do. He violated the family values and social conventions of his day by including women who were not members of his own family among his friends and disciples. He associated with dishonest businessmen, social outcasts, prostitutes, and religious heretics, who were despised and excluded by all the decent people of his time. It seems, in fact, that about the only people he did not love, accept, and welcome into his company were the moral, law-abiding, God-fearing people of his own religious community. *They* were his enemies; not so much because he excluded them as because they did not *want* to be included in the company of one who was the friend of the wrong kind of people. But he did not tell even these self-righteous insiders that they were left out of God's inclusive love. He said only that those who are now first will be last in the kingdom of God, and those who are now last will be first. For Jesus, the unqualified love of God included even those who rejected it.

In our time as well, to live in Jesus' company and to be his follower is to believe in and live by the good news of the love of God that includes rich and poor, male and female, moral and immoral, political liberals and conservatives, those who share our religious convictions and those who do not. And in our time, too, the greatest barrier to faithful proclamation of the good news— and the greatest barrier to others' hearing and believing it—is the self-righteous exclusiveness of insiders.

The Christian community is divided by competing groups of people on the Right and on the Left who are sure that their understanding of Christian faith and life is the correct one, and who openly or secretly exclude from their fellowship (and, by implication, from the inclusive love of God) those who do not believe and live as they do.

Some individuals and groups say or imply, "God loves, accepts, forgives, and welcomes you, but *we* don't—unless you agree with our evangelical or conservative interpretation of scripture; unless you are committed to a patriarchal, hierarchical understanding of God and human relationships in church and society; unless you believe that Jesus is the *only* way, truth, and life and Christianity the only true religion; unless you oppose socialism, liberalism, homosexuality, abortion, and everything else that destroys the moral fabric and family values of our society."

Others (paradoxically, often those for whom "inclusiveness" and "diversity" are the highest virtues) say, "God loves, accepts, forgives, and welcomes you, but *we* don't—if your interpretation of scripture is too 'literalistic' or too 'evangelical'; if you have a patriarchal, hierarchical understanding of God, family, and society; if you do not welcome and respect followers of other religions; if you would not welcome homosexual persons into full participation in the life and ministry of the Christian community;

if you are not pro-choice on the abortion issue and are not against the religious and political Right in general."

Still others are "moderates" who will have nothing to do with either the extreme Right or the extreme Left—and feel superior to both—though they are not always sure exactly where they themselves stand.

Insofar as all of us fit into one or another of these groups, we exclude not only others but also ourselves from the company of the Christ who welcomes outsiders, includes the excluded, loves the unlovable, and forgives sinners. If it were not for the inclusive love of God that includes even self-righteous Christians, there would be no hope for any of us!

What, then, would it mean to live by the good news of God's inclusive love? We would still have rigorous debates in the church about what is good and true and authentically Christian. But we would be modest about the correctness of people who are on "our side." We would be willing to learn from and be corrected by others, both inside and outside the church, who may see some consequences of authentic Christian faith and life that we have been unable or unwilling to see. Even when differences remain, we would seek to demonstrate, both in the church's own life and in the public policies that the church advocates, the love of God that includes and wills the common good of all people and all kinds of people, everywhere—no one excluded, everyone included.

God's Disciplining and Liberating Love

The good news is that while Jesus welcomed into his company all kinds of people, just as they were and whatever they had done or not done, he did not *leave* them as they were. He invited and commanded them to leave their old lives behind and to follow him in a new and dangerous life of costly discipleship that set them at odds with the values and norms of the world around them. At the same time, he offered them *freedom*: freedom *from* the self-enslavement of living however they pleased (since God was there to accept and forgive); freedom *from* the self-deception of living by confidence in their own moral and religious superiority (since God was on their side). He offered freedom *for* finding their true humanity in loving God and fellow human beings, freedom *for* living in joyful, thankful, and obedient anticipation of the coming reign of God's compassion and justice in and for the world.

The Shape of Discipleship

What would such obedient and free Christian discipleship look like in our time? I mention only two aspects of it that I believe our divided church most needs to remember.

1. The life of discipleship to which Jesus called the community of his followers claimed *every* area of their lives. He called them *both* to be faithful and responsible in their personal lives and family relationships *and* to bear witness to God's compassionate and just reign in and for the world.

In our divided church, however, we tend to make this both-and commission into an either-or alternative. Some Christians (mostly conservatives?) are deeply disturbed by the promiscuity, permissiveness, and moral relativism that they believe are rampant in both church and society. They tend to be so obsessed with this area that they ignore issues of the social, political, and economic justice God requires of us and are suspicious of those who concentrate on them. Others (mostly liberals?) are so committed to work for justice, freedom, and peace in the world that they tend to be indifferent toward the issue of faithfulness and responsibility not only in the personal and family lives of others but also in their own lives. To the extent that this is true (as conservatives charge), they actually do contribute to the permissiveness, promiscuity, and moral relativism that are indeed rampant not only in the world outside the church but also in the leadership and membership of the church itself.

If we were faithful followers of Jesus, we could not limit Christian discipleship to this or that area of life. We would be free for authentic discipleship that acknowledges his claim on, and integrates and renews, every area of our lives.

2. The life of discipleship to which Jesus called his followers

was the discipleship of *service*. He said that he came not to be served but to serve, and he told his followers that they, too, were called not to lord it over others but to be servants—servants of their servant Lord, servants of one another, and servants of the cause of God in the world.

Who among us does not believe that this applies to us, too? Yet the church is torn apart by factions that compete for the power to dominate and control fellow Christians and the church and to dictate to them what they can and cannot, must and must not, do and think. Some even try to gain enough support to influence the government to impose their moral standards, religious faith, and liberal or conservative social program on everyone *outside* the church.

What would it mean for us to follow Jesus as a community of *servant* disciples? I mention here only what I believe it would mean for the way in which we deal with two of the most controversial issues we fight about today.

A faithful community of followers of Jesus would invite and welcome into its fellowship all kinds of people, whatever their race, gender, sexual orientation, economic status, or cultural background. All would be invited and welcomed, not just to receive everything the church has to offer them and do for them but to find their places as servants in a servant community.

This invitation would carry with it both some strict requirements and freedom of opportunity. All members of the church would be required to demonstrate loving covenant faithfulness and responsibility in all their personal and familial relationships, as well as commitment to serve not just the interest of any one group in the church but the common good of the whole community. But all members would also be free to offer themselves and to be welcomed as potential candidates for any of the opportunities for service in the community, including positions as ordained and unordained leaders. Not all have the gifts and talents to qualify them for service in that (or any other) particular way. But a church which remembers that all Christians are invited to a life of disciplined Christian service would not exclude *anyone* from the possibility of pursuing any of the ways it provides for serving

God, the Christian community, and the world. To do so would be for the church to deprive itself of the unique contribution some could make to its life and mission. Worse yet, it would prevent some from answering the call to servant discipleship that comes from the servant Lord himself.

In the public sphere, the servant community of followers of Jesus would exercise the same costly and free discipleship that is required of them and given to them in their individual lives and in the Christian community. Knowing that their servant Lord invites them to serve and not to dominate and control, they would give up and oppose all attempts by the church or government to impose Christian or biblical faith and life on everyone else. Knowing that they are called to serve *Jesus Christ*, they would resist every attempt from within or outside the church to put the community of his followers in the service of any conservative or liberal party or ideology. (The church would be neither the Republican nor the Democratic Party at prayer.)

Then they would be free—free not to withdraw from the public arena but to ask and be open to learn what their crucified and risen Lord is saying and doing in the world, and what they have to say and do in his service. In a pluralistic society, they could not appeal directly to the Bible, the will of God, or Jesus Christ to defend the positions they take. But, given the alternatives and possibilities that are available to them, they would support those that most clearly point in the direction of the coming reign of God that Jesus proclaimed and embodied. They would, for instance, support public policies and legislation that look out especially for the health and welfare of the poor and excluded; defend the common good against self- and community-destructive individualism; promote truth telling and promise keeping in personal relationships as well as in business and government; advocate a justice system that seeks reconciliation, rehabilitation, and restoration rather than retribution, vengeance, and destruction for those who have made themselves the enemies of society.

Such a strategy might seem too liberal to some conservatives in church and society, because it would work for public policy that only indirectly reflects the requirements of Christian faith and life instead of trying to impose them on others in a pluralistic society. It might seem too conservative to some liberals, because it would openly and unapologetically seek to bring faith in the servant lordship of Jesus Christ to bear on public life. Even if the Christian community were to agree on the strategy itself, there would still be disagreement and arguments about which alternatives and decisions best reflect the will and work of God in a particular time, place, and situation. But it would be a strategy that could make a uniquely and genuinely Christian contribution to public discourse about what a just and humane society in a pluralistic world should look like.

Back to Where We Began

We ought not to talk too cynically about what Christians and the Christian community "would" do "if they were" to bear faithful witness to the good news of the inclusive and disciplining/liberating love of God. Sometimes, here and there, now and then, by the grace of God in a living Christ and by the renewing power of his Holy Spirit, they actually do it (even in a divided and bickering church). But even if we look at the church at its very best, it is clear that the good news is not about what we Christians and our church are, say, and do—or what we *could* be and say and do, if only the right group in the church could have its way. The good news is who the living God is, whom we have come to know in Jesus of Nazareth, and what this God has done, is doing, and promises to do in and for the world, with or without the help and cooperation of God's people. Only *this* good news can save us from the frustration, doubt, disillusionment, and despair that inevitably come when we depend on our own resources and ability to overcome all the suffering, evil, injustice, and death in our own broken lives, our broken church, and our broken world. Only *this* good news can give us the energy and courage to live in stubborn and hopeful anticipation of the reign of God—and the new humanity in a new heaven and earth—that nevertheless, despite all evidence to the contrary, are already on the way and surely will come.

Jesus Christ as Host and Guest

Amy Plantinga Pauw

Divine and Human Hospitality

God hosts us in the world. From our first breath to our last, God welcomes us into a life-giving and life-sustaining network of relations with the physical world, with various human communities, and with God's own self. God's all-embracing hospitality is the presupposition for every aspect of our lives—physical, social, and spiritual. Even before we knock, God graciously opens the door for us. Even before we ask for food, God spreads a table before us. The creative, redemptive, sustaining love of God takes the shape of extravagant hospitality toward all creation. We are intended to live joyfully and generously, assured of God's gracious abundance.

But in a world of injustice and alienation, divine hospitality is hard to trust and harder still to emulate. The fear of scarcity replaces the assurance of abundance. The role of host can seem too difficult or dangerous to undertake. Hospitality becomes pinched, and the needs of guests go unrecognized and unmet. Or hospitality becomes twisted so that it serves the interests of the host and becomes a burden to the guests. In this kind of world, extravagant hospitality becomes a scandal.

Perhaps it is not surprising, then, that the scandal of extrava-

12

gant hospitality is one of the clearest hallmarks of Jesus' life and teaching. One of the first things others notice about him is that he eats with tax collectors and sinners! Table fellowship with all the wrong sorts of people is a dominant pattern in Jesus' ministry. He provides excellent wine for a wedding and feeds crowds of thousands on the hillside. When Jesus says, "I have come to call not the righteous but sinners" (Matt. 9:13), he uses a word that means "call to a meal" or "invite." "Everything is ready! Come to the banquet!" (see Matthew 22) sums up his gospel message. The Last Supper stands as a culmination of a ministry of hospitality, in which the bread that is blessed, broken, and given to the world is Christ himself. Jesus, the Bread of Life, becomes both host and meal, giving his own body and blood for the life of the world. In Jesus Christ we see one who trusts in God's hospitality to the whole world and perfectly incarnates it in his own life.

Resurrection faith hopes for the fulfillment of God's extravagant hospitality in a world without mourning or crying or pain. Scripture hints at the cosmic scope of this fulfillment, at a day when even the wolf and the lamb, the lion and the ox, will eat together; when no creature will hurt or destroy another (Isaiah 65). One of the most pervasive images of human salvation in scripture is the banquet table, with God serving as generous host. Salvation is feasting in the kingdom of God, where people will come from north, south, east, and west to sit at table together. Their celebration will satisfy the yearnings of body and spirit. Their fellowship will shatter boundaries of language and culture and past enmity. In Jesus' fellowship meals, in the homes of Pharisees or of Gentiles, surrounded by thousands or alone with his disciples, hints of this joyful communion begin to heal the pain and brokenness of human life. His followers glimpse the glorious end that awaits them: feasting together in God's new realm.

But at the center of the Christian story is also a startling reversal of roles: in Jesus Christ, God comes to dwell among us as guest. Jesus' life narrates the presence of God-with-us in scandalously vulnerable ways: as a homeless baby; as an adult with no place to lay his head; as a convict, abandoned and scorned by others. He epitomizes the needy stranger, dependent on the hospitality of others. He asks for hospitality from a Samaritan woman (John 4) and a rich tax collector (Luke 19) and receives it gladly from many others. In their hospitality to "the least" among them, his disciples from all times and places continue to discover that they are hosting their Lord. God comes in Christ as generous and gracious host but also as needy and grateful guest.

Is this really good news? Could this party giver be the one we had hoped would redeem Israel? Is receiving the hospitality of sinners any way to triumph over the evil powers of the world? The scandal of Jesus Christ as extravagant host and needy guest prompts John the Baptist's question: "Are you the one who is to come, or are we to wait for another?" (Luke 7:20). Behind the question is what Barbara Brown Taylor calls the crashing disillusionment felt by everyone "who looks for a Lord who does not come, or who does not come in the way he was expected":

> The Messiah was supposed to change things. He was supposed to burn up all the human trash and dead wood of the world. He was supposed to come with a sharp ax, with a gleaming pitchfork, and separate the good guys from the bad guys once and for all. He was supposed to clean up the world, so that people like Herod were no longer in power and people like John were no longer in prison, but Jesus has utterly failed to meet John's expectations.[1]

Instead, we find a Messiah who specializes in hospitality to "spiritual weaklings and moral misfits." We find a Messiah who hungers and thirsts and seeks the fellowship and nurture of others. In his openness to suffering and rejection, Jesus Christ as host and guest defies John's expectations, and perhaps ours as well. Giving and receiving hospitality seems like a terribly roundabout way of saving the world.

To be sure, there is a kind of hospitality that fits with John's hopes for a dramatic separation of good folks from bad folks. There are smug fellowships of the righteous to which no sinners need apply. There are victory celebrations to which no losers are invited. There are feasts of vengeance at which host and guests rejoice that their enemies have finally received what they deserved. The eschatological counterpart to this triumphalist, exclusive hospitality is parodied in a little rhyme:

> We are the Lord's elected few; let all the rest be damned.
> There's room enough in hell for you; we won't have heaven
> crammed.

These visions of hospitality, both earthly and heavenly, were no doubt as prevalent in Jesus' day as they are in ours. Assembling the guest list for such a banquet requires identifying the good people who deserve to be invited and excluding the bad people who do not.

In his parables about the kingdom of God in Matthew 22 and Luke 14, Jesus takes this all-too-common mode of human hospitality and turns it on its head. He compares God's kingdom to a banquet to which respectable, deserving people have been invited. But inexplicably, they all reject the invitation, and the angry host calls for the disrespectable and undeserving to take their place. These parables are not an analogue to Jesus' earthly practice of hospitality, which embraced respectable Pharisees and disrespectable sinners alike, sometimes at the same meal (Luke 7). Nor is the principal function of these outrageous parables to prophesy future, eschatological events or to promise salvation to Gentile "sinners." Instead, they deliberately portray the inconceivable, in a sharp warning to the "children of the kingdom" to heed Jesus' call to salvation and repentance. His invitation presents them with a choice: by accepting his hospitality, they renounce their claims to be the righteous, deserving ones. Jesus' provocation in these parables is aimed at all those who pride themselves on their religious virtue—whether that virtue is one of high moral standards or of winsome inclusivity. Jesus comes to call sinners, not the righteous (Mark 2), and there is more than one form of righteousness that can get in the way of receiving God's hospitality.

"Come, Lord Jesus, be our guest" a familiar children's prayer begins. Believing the good news of Jesus Christ means receiving his hospitality. It means dwelling in the place he has lovingly prepared for us (John 14). But it also means receiving him as guest, so that Christ may dwell in our hearts through faith (Ephesians 3). God graciously hosts us but also desires for us, as a community of faith, to be host, to become together a living temple of the Holy Spirit (1 Corinthians 6). Believing the good news is about entering into the interplay of divine hospitality.

Responding to the divine request for hospitality requires both interior transformation and outward patterns of action. It means accepting God's gracious hospitality to us. And it means opening our hearts to God as a dwelling place and offering hospitality to the needy strangers in whom Jesus comes to us. What is that going to look like in the concrete messiness of everyday life?[2] Here we cannot rest content with easy platitudes about trusting God and accepting everybody just as Jesus did. Both the witness of scripture and the realities of the human condition are too complex for a "What would Jesus do?" ethic. To understand divine hospitality and our appropriate hospitable response requires first taking a difficult detour into divine and human inhospitality.

Divine Inhospitality

Just as the banquet table is one of the most glorious images of God's salvation in scripture, the refusal of table fellowship is one of the most haunting images of divine judgment. In Isaiah 65, God taunts the faithless in Israel, saying, "My servants shall eat, but you shall be hungry; my servants shall drink, but you shall be thirsty; my servants shall rejoice, but you shall be put to shame" (Isa. 65:13). The theme of divine inhospitality permeates some of the best-known passages in scripture: the psalmist says of God, "You prepare a table before me in the presence of my enemies" (Ps. 23:5), who, presumably, stand hungrily by. In the Magnificat, Mary proclaims that the Lord "has filled the hungry with good things, and sent the rich away empty" (Luke 1:53). The book of Revelation provides one of most vivid images of divine judgment in all of scripture, with its horrifying caricature of the "marriage supper of the Lamb":

With a loud voice [an angel] called to all the birds that fly in
midheaven, 'Come, gather for the great supper of God, to eat
the flesh of kings, the flesh of captains, the flesh of the
mighty, the flesh of horses and their riders—flesh of all, both
free and slave, both small and great.' . . . [A]nd all the birds
were gorged with their flesh. (Rev. 19:17–18, 21b)

With unnerving regularity, the "yes" of God's hospitality to
some is paired with the "no" of exclusion to others.

The theme of exclusion also runs through the teachings of
Jesus. The depictions of God's inhospitality in the banquet parables are even more shocking than the indiscriminate hospitality
to the undeserving. Not only does the host invite the poor, the
crippled, the blind, and the lame as substitute guests, he also
vows that "none of those who were invited will taste my dinner"
(Luke 14:24). Having spurned their invitation, the original banquet guests are now excluded from the feast and thrown into the
outer darkness, where there is weeping and gnashing of teeth
(Matthew 22). The kingdom banquet is scandalous not only in
whom it includes but also in whom it excludes. Likewise, in the
Sermon on the Mount, Jesus warns that some with his name on
their lips and many deeds of power on their résumés will be told,
"I never knew you; go away from me, you evildoers" (Matt. 7:23).
Any celebration of Jesus' extravagant hospitality must reckon
with the shadow cast by his threats of ultimate inhospitality.

The theme of divine exclusion in scripture is troubling—it is
meant to be. But it is crucial not to cut scriptural images of
divine inhospitality loose from their moorings in communal faith
practices. Passages warning about God's ultimate inhospitality to
some people are neither a reliable guide to eschatological events
nor an invitation to the faithful to help prune the guest list for
the eschatological banquet. These difficult teachings function
rather as a warning or encouragement to particular faith communities in their own practices of hospitality. They are meant to
provoke our hospitable response, not to define our future hopes
or model appropriate human behavior.

Often the theme of divine inhospitality in scripture functions
to relativize and restrain human impulses to inhospitality. The
people banished to outer darkness in Matthew's Gospel are not

the ones we would expect to end up there, not the sort of people whom we would be tempted to exclude. Rather, Jesus' teaching provides no reinforcement to self-righteous hospitality. There is a similar shock of reversal in the parable of Lazarus and the rich man in Luke 16. In his life on earth, Lazarus was excluded from the privileges and pleasures of the rich man's table. Lacking the privacy and protection that wealth affords, Lazarus was powerless to exclude even the dogs that came to lick his sores. That all-too-familiar picture of inhospitality by the privileged and coerced hospitality by the destitute is powerfully subverted by the eschatological inhospitality experienced by the rich man in Hades.

Sometimes scriptural images of divine inhospitality goad the faithful by warning of the dangers of responding to God with inhospitable indifference or violence. God's invitation to abundant life is a serious matter. If our hands are so full with God's material blessings that we are oblivious to God's presence in the world and fail to provide welcome to those in whom God comes to us, we bring down divine judgment on ourselves. "Lord, when was it that we saw you hungry or thirsty or a stranger or naked or sick or in prison, and did not take care of you?" the hapless goats ask (Matt. 25:44). We never noticed; we were too busy; we did not want to take the risk. Feeding Christ's lambs seems like such a troublesome way to demonstrate our faith. But John's Gospel declares that it is inseparable from loving Christ and having God make a home with us (John 14, 21). The eschatological warnings of divine exclusion reflect the urgency of a hospitable response to God, a "saying yes" to God that transforms our relationships both to God and to neighbor.

In sum, warnings of God's inhospitality in scripture do not function to corroborate our own inhospitable impulses and acts. We are not to hear Jesus' teachings about divine exclusion and "go and do likewise." As disciples, we are called to feed Christ's lambs, not to banish unworthy guests from the banquet hall. There are profound disjunctions between God's inhospitality and ours. Yet we sometimes have to be inhospitable. Human inhospitality is inevitable and at times necessary, because limited human beings cannot offer limitless hospitality. Even at its best, our hospitality is only a pale reflection of God's hospitality, and our inhospitality to some does not negate the wideness of God's hospitable mercy to them. In discerning the shape of human hospitality that appropriately responds to the extravagant hospitality of God, we need also to look honestly at the legitimate reasons for human inhospitality.

Hospitality and Its Limits

Human hospitality, unlike God's, is obviously limited by constraints of time, resources, energy, and geography. We cannot be hospitable to everyone, everywhere, at every time. In discerning our capacity for hospitality, the physical limits and emotional needs of our entire community must be considered. Offering hospitality to strangers can exacerbate the vulnerability of less-powerful persons in the host community. A flagrant example of this is found in Genesis 19, where, in an effort to protect his two guests, Lot is willing to sacrifice the well-being of his daughters. Offering hospitality to the stranger can intensify unjust relations within the host community. Women and servants, for example, often bear most of the burden of offering hospitality. Children of hosts sometimes go hungry so that important guests will be well fed. Extravagant hospitality to others cannot be pursued at the cost of neglecting or abusing "the least" among us.

Human hospitality is also hampered by our vulnerability to external threat. We rightly seek security and protection against destructive forces. The biblical narrative abounds with broad injunctions to show hospitality to the stranger. But at various points it also recognizes that the world can pose a grave threat to the children of God. This recognition is especially apparent in the Israelite community after the exile and in the Johannine community of early Christians. In a world of violence and falsehood, the hospitality of the community of faith tends to turn inward, excluding those who threaten its integrity and well-being. The stranger in the community's midst is sent home, and the stranger at the door is denied entry. "Do not receive into the house or welcome anyone who comes to you and does not bring this teaching," 2 John counsels, "for to welcome is to participate in the evil deeds of such a person" (2 John 10–11). Johannine hospitality is concrete and generous, but its exclusive purpose is to bind the members of the community with one another and with God.

In circumstances of extreme vulnerability, this may be a necessary stance for people of faith to take. There are times when we must resist offering hospitality to certain persons because of their destructive powers, when we are called instead to pray that God will show them hospitality while delivering us from them. The gospel injunction to love our enemies does not always coincide with the command to offer them hospitality. We can affirm that God continues to be loving host to the larger world, even when we as the people of God dare not emulate this divine hospitality.

But a Christian hospitality turned in on itself is at best a provisional strategy, and a morally dangerous one at that. Allan Boesak has chronicled how the refusal of white Reformed Christians in South Africa to share the Lord's Table with their black brothers and sisters was initially justified on account of their own prejudice or "weakness," as it came to be called. But soon the theology of apartheid led to "the acceptance, the idealization, and institutionalization of that brokenness."[3] Refusing the hospitality of the Lord's Table to blacks was eventually seen as a participation in God's will for the church. What starts as an inability to express God's love for the world can become a denial of that love. We always make the decision to exclude as morally compromised creatures; our sense of physical or moral weakness remains a temptation to a sectarian hospitality that recognizes God's hospitality only to people like ourselves. We are all at risk of falling into Jonah's predicament, begrudging God's yes to our enemies and finding God's gracious hospitality toward them displeasing.

The recognition of our own moral weakness is also a brake on our capacity to receive hospitality from others. Not every offer of hospitality is life-giving. Proverbs 9 depicts two invitations to hospitality. One is given by Woman Wisdom, who sets her table and calls out to all the simple to come and eat and drink and share in her wisdom. The other is issued by Woman Folly, who also calls to the simple to draw near, but her water is poison and her bread is death. To accept her invitation is to forsake the life Wisdom offers and to dwell among the dead. One invitation must be refused. As the apostle Paul insists, "You cannot drink the cup of the Lord and the cup of demons. You cannot partake of the table of the Lord and the table of demons" (1 Cor. 10:21). Inside each of us are things that could grow into hell, into a fundamental stance of inhospitality toward God and neighbor. Part of faith's discernment is to reject the hospitality of people who may nurture these impulses in us. Like the prophet Daniel who refused to eat the king's sumptuous food, we must refuse some invitations to hospitality as a matter of conscience.

The Banquet Vision

Human limitations—physical, emotional, and moral—impose limits on the hospitality we can offer and receive from others. Precisely because our rationales for inhospitality are based on human weakness, however, we must resist claiming divine authority for them. While we must continue saying no to hospitality to some people, we must be very wary of claiming God's blessing on it. Human inhospitality does not necessarily coincide with divine inhospitality. Our temporal exclusion of some does not imply their eschatological exclusion from the heavenly banquet. God's hospitality reaches out to those to whom our hospitality cannot or even should not extend. This means that our exclusion of others is always in brackets, always provisional, always ready to be overturned by the surprising graciousness of God.

The tradition of the welcoming table, prevalent among Southern black churches but not unique to them, provides a striking example of how joyful, grace-filled hospitality can break down the dividing walls of human hostility. At these fellowship dinners, held on the church grounds, a large meal is prepared for everyone who would come, rich and poor, black and white. In a "pigmentocracy" such as the American South, in which legal measures to prevent people of different races from eating together or even sharing a water fountain were brutally enforced, the welcoming table was a powerful witness to God's extravagant hospitality.

For the Christian civil rights activist Fannie Lou Hamer, the welcoming table was a foreshadowing of the kingdom banquet. During the freedom struggle, the welcoming table brought together black Christians and the young Jewish volunteers for the Freedom Summer project, whom Hamer described as "the best friends we ever met." Food generously offered and gratefully received strengthened the bonds of their shared commitment to a new community. Astoundingly, Hamer was able to recognize that even segregationists such as Ross Barnett and James O. Eastland would be welcome at the table, provided they "learn some manners." "It wouldn't solve any problem for me to hate whites just because they hate me," she declared.[4] In a society filled with hatred and fear, the welcoming table provided a glimpse of the healing, justice, and peace that would make it possible for the peoples of the earth to sit down at the banquet table together and rejoice in God's gracious abundance.

We are always "following at a distance" when we attempt to reflect the goodness and generosity of the welcoming God of Jesus Christ. Christian efforts at hospitality cannot rely on human strength alone if the awkward, difficult, risky work of welcoming the stranger is to be sustained. God's grace, made perfect in weakness, works through us so that we can be channels of God's hospitality to others despite our vulnerabilities and shortcomings. Through the same grace, we are able to acknowledge our own neediness and gratefully accept God's hospitality offered to us through our neighbors.

Part of the scandal of Jesus Christ as generous host and needy guest is the scandal of a divine love that dares to be so vulnerable to suffering and rejection. In genuine human hospitality, these vulnerabilities are never completely absent. But another part of the scandalous good news is the scandal of divine joy. We prefer our joy in moderate, bite-sized amounts. The full joy that the hospitality of God promises us overwhelms our narrow capacities. Just as the joy of a new child requires a lot of stretching and accommodating, by her mother during her gestation and birth and later by her family and friends and the larger community of which she becomes a part, so the joy God intends for us will not leave our routines and boundaries undisturbed.[5] Entering into the interplay of receiving and giving hospitality now is a preparation for the joy of the eschatological banquet. As David Ford affirms, "wholehearted feasting together" is the eschatological joy which God promises us. "The resurrected Jesus invites us to savor this in advance and to create now in the present signs that this is the true reality."[6] Believing the good news of Jesus Christ requires living into joy!

NOTES

1. Barbara Brown Taylor, "The Gift of Disillusionment," in *God in Pain: Teaching Sermons on Suffering* (Nashville: Abingdon Press, 1998), 18, 20.
2. For a persuasive account of the difficulties and blessings of the Christian practice of hospitality, see Christine D. Pohl, *Making Room: Recovering Hospitality as a Christian Practice* (Grand Rapids: Wm. B. Eerdmans Publishing Co., 1999).
3. Allan Boesak, *Black and Reformed: Apartheid, Liberation and the Calvinist Tradition* (Maryknoll, N.Y.: Orbis Books, 1984), 89–90.
4. Quoted in Charles Marsh, *God's Long Summer: Stories of Faith and Civil Rights* (Princeton, N.J.: Princeton University Press, 1997), 22, 45–46.
5. David F. Ford, *The Shape of Living: Spiritual Directions for Everyday Life* (Grand Rapids: Baker Book House, 1997), 186.
6. Ibid.

The Narrow Door

Luke 13:22–30; Isaiah 43:1–7

Jon M. Walton

A few summers ago I was in Europe, and as all tourists do, I visited several of the innumerable castles that are there. But after a while one castle starts to look like another, no matter what country you're in or in what period the castle was built.

There was one in particular, however, that I remember very well. It was the one with the maze.

Whoever built the castle thought that, as a protective device as well as an entertainment, he would build a very complicated labyrinth of hedges, a puzzle that has been carefully tended and meticulously groomed all through the centuries. Over time the hedges have grown to about eight or nine feet high, tall enough to prevent you from getting your bearings once inside.

I thought I could probably knock off that maze in about five minutes, and I said as much to the attendant at the entrance as I went in. He was European, stuffy, and not amused. From his look I suspected he had seen my kind go in that maze and never come out again.

The first part wasn't too hard, a left here, a right there. It was going rather well, I thought—except, of course, I kept hitting blind alleys. Soon I found I was passing people in both directions who looked vaguely familiar to me.

I began to get a little concerned after about a half an hour or so, when I heard voices on the other side of the hedges that seemed to come and then go.

It became more and more frustrating the longer I searched. I started to imagine that nightfall would come and I would still be there, trying to make my way by moonlight.

At last the attendant from the entrance came up to me, doing what must have been one of his hourly sweeps of the lost. "Having trouble are we?" he asked, trying to keep his face straight. "Just follow me," he said. "It's by the narrow way."

And sure enough, there was a kind of gap in the hedges that served as the narrow door to the last row leading to the exit. And standing sideways you could make it through and be on your way. But for those unaccustomed to mazes or to risking a slightly different way of solving the puzzle, the solution for getting out proved too difficult to resolve.

It was as I was leaving the maze that I discovered the attendant was a Christian, as he paraphrased Jesus. "Don't feel bad," he said smugly, "many have tried, few are able."

I cannot help but think of that castle and of that maze when I hear Jesus' words "Strive to enter through the narrow door; for many, I tell you, will try to enter and will not be able."

The teaching comes in response to a question posed by someone along the way as Jesus traveled through one town and village after another. It was an earnest question, not hostile but seeking: "Lord, will only a few be saved?"

What a great question! And wouldn't we like to know! John Calvin loved this one. It led him into those magnificent statements about the sovereignty of God and on to his theology about predestination, picking up speed to double predestination, until finally, at warp speed, he went right into a brick wall as free will and God's sovereignty collided.

"Lord, will only a few be saved!" What a good question. We are still asking it. The minimalists and New Age folks of our spiritual reawakening in this country smear it all around saying, "Oh, it doesn't make any difference what you believe. We're all going to the same place." They seem to say, "All will be saved." But is it that simple?

Some in our culture dismiss the question of salvation by

suggesting that it's essentially irrelevant. God is like some all-permeating gas in the universe, they say, impersonal and distant, unknowable. With an impersonal God, who needs salvation?

Still others are looking for a form of salvation in a bottle or at the end of a needle or in a powder up the nose—an expedient and sensory answer to an eternal and spiritual yearning. There is no salvation there, at least no salvation in the Hebrew sense of wholeness, health, oneness, and peace with God.

"Lord, will only a few be saved!" A simple yes or no would do. But instead, Jesus answers enigmatically, "Strive to enter through the narrow door; for many, I tell you, will try to enter and will not be able."

So how do we get to it, to that narrow door of salvation that many strive to enter but few are able to find?

Is the narrow door asceticism, the monastic life? Do you have to take vows to find it? Must you live a life like Mother Teresa or endure martyrdom like Martin Luther King Jr.? How do we get to the narrow door and, once there, enter?

Maybe this is all easier than we make it, with our discussions of determinism and free will and grace. Maybe we all know where that narrow door is. Maybe we've always known. After all, there are certain well-traveled routes that just about all of us along the theological spectrum, whether Presbyterian Coalition people or Covenant Network people or "normal" people in between, can affirm.

Paul told the Ephesians and us how to do it: "[L]ead a life worthy of the calling to which you have been called, with all humility and gentleness, with patience, bearing with one another in love, making every effort to maintain the unity of the Spirit in the bond of peace" (Eph. 4:1–3). Somewhere at the end of that king of journey is a door worth entering.

Maybe you get to the narrow door simply by leading a life of Christian discipline—you know, trying to live the Christian life as best you can, nothing too fancy about it.

You pray every day and you read your Bible. You go to church, get your children baptized. You keep the Ten Commandments in your heart and in your life as well as you are able. You treat people with respect and attempt in some imperfect way to love one another as Christ has loved us. You become race- and color-blind and start to see others with the delight in which God has made all of us, so different. You care for the poor and work for justice in this world of injustice.

You make solemn vows to the person you love and try with all your heart not to turn away. And if you have made no such promises, you try with all your heart to be responsible in your living, not to squander your love or your body but to use it wisely and carefully, knowing that the heart is a fragile thing and our bodies are given to us imprinted with the very image of God on them and in them, something to be treasured and honored in its keeping.

You do all those things trying to find your way to the narrow door, all the time knowing that nothing you ever do *earns* you the right of passage once you get there. Surprise of surprises, it is always and only by the love and grace of God that any of us ever find the door or enter through it. And as often as not, somebody has to come and rescue us and take us there when we are lost and giving up hope of finding it.

Just about all of us in this church of ours, or better said, this church of Jesus Christ's, hold those things in common, and would that it could take us all the way home.

But somehow it does not, and we are left divided by our disparate understandings of how gracious is God's grace and how inclusive is God's welcome. God help us, our enmity over the *Book of Order*'s G-6.0106b is so strong that it tends to make friends enemies, which only makes the journey to that narrow door longer and lonelier.

It has gotten so bad that some are saying we do not even share a common faith anymore in our church, which, if it were true, would be the greatest tragedy of all.

We do know that the trials are mounting in the church as in the Synod of the Northeast, and this is causing sessions and pastor nominating committees to inquire about bedroom behavior and whether our sexual expression is faithful or unfaithful, active or inactive, self-acknowledged or self-denying, frequent or infrequent. I feel more and more anxious about all this, not because I have so much incriminating evidence to report but because I have so little.

We are, as a denomination, right now hell-bent on getting to some narrow way—so narrow, I fear, that none of us may make it. I find myself wondering with the psalmist, "O Lord, if thou shouldest mark iniquities (as do my brothers and sisters in the church), O Lord who shall stand?"

I think I am most concerned about the idea that the narrow way to salvation leads us to love the sinner while we hate the sin.

The problem is that none of us is very good at loving sinners and hating their sins at the same time. Hate has a way of enveloping everything, and so . . . Matthew Shepherd was tied to a Wyoming fence rail and left to die like a trophy animal in the winter cold. And Barry Winchell, twenty-one years old, an army private, was murdered at Fort Campbell, Kentucky, this past summer, bludgeoned to death with a baseball bat while he lay sleeping—by fellow soldiers yelling, "Faggot!" I think we have enough already of loving the sinner and hating the sin!

In the Gospel reading a surprising reversal takes place, one that puts us all on warning.

People arrive at the door and it is night. God, who is thinly veiled as the householder in the story, is roused from sleep and comes down to answer.

But he is not quick to open. "How do I know you?" he asks.

"We ate and drank with you. You taught in our streets," they say. "We talked about you all the time. We prayed, we tithed, we contributed to the building fund, we taught in the church school. We did everything the way you'd have wanted it.

"We kept folks out that didn't belong in the church—the tax collectors and prostitutes, the drug addicts, the radical feminists, the gays and lesbians. Those people from east and west and north and south, the Gentiles, the great unwashed. We kept them out. We forbade them office. We did it for you, Master. We did it for you."

But the master, unimpressed by the claims, responds from behind the closed door, "I do not where you come from."

Fred Craddock says of this reversal of expectations that "added to the pain of sitting before a closed door will be the sight of large numbers who are admitted . . . [who are] the unexpected Gentiles who heard and believed," the ones everybody knew could not enter the kingdom.[1]

What Jesus wants us to know and we are loath to get is that in the kingdom of heaven, God alone is arbiter of who will be called to serve and who will not, who is in and who is out, and who will be left outside pounding on the door. To assume that place of judgment that is God's place is a terrible mistake. *And it cuts both ways.*

What we all need to understand is that in the kingdom of heaven, we will be sitting with folks we did not expect would be there. The place cards will be surprising: you know, John Buchanan next to Jerry Andrews; Joanna Adams next to Roberta Hestenes; Chris Glaser next to Clayton Bell. And if I get in, I get to sit next to that elder in my church who for all these years just hasn't gotten it, the one who always wants to tighten things up.

But, you know, it'll be right. It will be wonderful to be there together. Because at last we will understand, even as we have been fully understood.

Some day we are going to understand that gay and straight alike, we all want essentially the same things in life: not promiscuity but constancy, not faithlessness but faithfulness, not to waste our lives on something of the moment but to give ourselves to something of eternity.

Don't we all want to build a home with light shining through the windows so brightly that many a friend and sometimes a stranger may find a welcome there? to know that another's heart beats for us somewhere? to live knowing that God has made us and delights in us just as we are? to believe that in this vast universe we have a place, and that we belong, and that God means for us good? Don't we all want to believe that Jesus includes us when he says, "Anyone who comes to me, I will in no wise cast out"?

Fred Buechner says that "salvation is an experience first and a doctrine second."[2] It is the experience of losing yourself and, by doing so, finding yourself. It is loving God and getting lost in that love so deeply that in it you are found.

It comes down to this: Anne Lamott, in her book *Traveling Mercies* (which I find myself quoting all the time), remembers a moment that had a touch of eternity in it, when the narrow door opened and two friends she watched entered in. It is the story of a member of her church named Ranola and of a man with AIDS named Ken. Lamott writes:

> Shortly after [Ken] started coming [to church], his partner died of the disease. A few weeks later Ken told us that right after Brandon died, Jesus had slid into the hole in his heart that Brandon's loss left, and had been there ever since. Ken has a totally lopsided face, ravaged and emaciated, but when he smiles, he is radiant. He looks like God's crazy nephew Phil. He says that he would gladly pay any price for what he has now, which is Jesus, and us.[3]

Lamott says Ranola, a large, beautiful black woman, kept her distance from Ken and always looked at him with confusion when she looked at him at all. She was raised in the South by Baptists, and she had been taught that Ken's way of life—that Ken—was an abomination.

One particular Sunday just before he died, Ken was very weak; he had had a stroke, and his face was more lopsided than ever. But he came to church, and during the prayers of the people, he spoke joyously of his life and decline, of grace and redemption, of how safe and happy he felt nonetheless.

The first hymn that day was "Jacob's Ladder." "Every rung goes higher, higher," the congregation sang. And Ken, who had not the strength to stand, sat and sang anyway, with the hymnal in his lap.

And then they sang, "His Eye Is on the Sparrow." And Anne Lamott says that Ken remained seated, too weak to stand on his own while the congregation stood around him:

> "Why should I feel discouraged? Why do the shadows fall?" [the congregation sang]. . . . Ranola watched Ken rather skeptically for a moment, and then her face began to melt

and contort like this, and she went to his side and bent down to lift him up–lifted up this white rag doll, this scarecrow. She held him next to her, draped over and against her like a child while they sang. And it pierced me.[4]

Salvation is an experience first and a doctrine second. It is loving God and getting lost in that love so deeply that in it you are found, and in it we find one another.

Strive, then, to enter through the narrow door; for many, I tell you, will try and will not be able.

NOTES

1. Fred Craddock, *Luke, Interpretation: A Bible Commentary for Teaching and Preaching* (Louisville, Ky.: Westminster John Knox Press, 1990), 172.
2. Frederick Buechner, *Wishful Thinking* (New York: Harper & Row, 1973), 84.
3. Anne Lamott, *Traveling Mercies: Some Thoughts on Faith* (New York: Pantheon Books, 1999), 64.
4. Ibid., 65.

was already dead. But Jesus said to the child's father, "Do not fear, only believe." And together they went to the house, which was already awash in the tears of the professional mourners who had gathered. The whole place was cluttered with grief, gossip, crepe hanging, and curiosity. The first thing Jesus did was clear out the house, reducing the situation to its life-and-death essence. Then he "took the child's father and mother and those who were with him" to the child, and breaking another religious taboo—the prohibition against touching the dead—"he took her by the hand and said to her, . . . 'Little girl, get up.' And immediately the girl got up and began to walk about. . . . At this [those present] were overcome with amazement." The ultimate barrier, the one between the living and the dead, had been broken. Jesus strictly ordered them not to speak of what they had seen, lest the meaning of it be misconstrued as magic rather than as the sign that the coming of the kingdom of God brings about radical reversals. Then he said, "Get this girl something to eat." Imagine: delivered from the deathbed to the dinner table; restored to wholeness and to community through barrier-breaking, life-giving power of God, present in Jesus.

How can one not love these three characters, these two stories folded in on one another like bright ribbons of hope? I love the reality check they provide: that regardless of one's status or place in the world, we are all in this business of human life together. Whether one is a fry cook, a patient with AIDS, a symphony conductor, or a CEO, there are times in every person's life when present realities make a mockery of the promises of God. A time will come when we have tried everything, and nothing seems to work; when it appears as if the only reasonable thing to do is to resign ourselves to the diagnosis of hopelessness. These two shining stories promise that because of the responsive nature of God, there are other options.

A desperate man boldly begs Jesus for help. Jesus answers, "Yes, I will come and do what I can." A desperate woman comes up behind him and timidly touches his cloak. He responds spontaneously again. Responsiveness is obviously an innate part of the nature of God, made manifest in God's own Son. It is an innate part of God's nature to act, to care, to respond to those who will ask in faith. How prone we are to think of God in stained-glass-window terms—still, distant, cold, much too holy to mess with my miseries. But the Jesus we meet in the Gospel of Mark is one willing to get up to his elbows in situations that appear to be beyond help.

Jesus' response is both immediate and indiscriminate. The marginalized person is just as worthy of Jesus' attention as the most prominent one. In the eyes of God, everyone is important. The blessings of his kingdom belong to all.

These stories have much to tell us about God, but I believe that they have as much or more to tell us about the way *to* God. At least for me, they are a reassurance that there is more than one way for human beings to come to God. For Jairus, the way was direct. He needed God's help. He came and asked for it outright. The unnamed woman also believed and also hoped, but she was unsure of herself, uncertain of her place and of her right to ask for anything. Timidly, unobtrusively, she reached out in search of a different future for herself.

I think about how it is with us and how some of us come to God by the way of Jairus, but I also think of how many of us come like the unnamed woman, a little more tentatively, sitting out of the way, in the balcony, perhaps. We come in the hope that we will find something real here. Something powerful. Something life-giving. Something that will help us become whole in a way we wish we were and need to be and have tried to be but are not yet. The great news of the story of the unnamed woman is that we can receive the blessing of Christ in her way as well. Some sit on the front row, know all the words to the hymns, and can name the deepest needs of their hearts in their prayers. But others struggle to find the melody, search for the words. Both paths lead to the heart of God—wholeness, peace, life, the real thing, hope as we face the thousands of little deaths that constitute human existence. Who does not long for these things?

In J. M. Coetzee's *Age of Iron*, a beautiful novel set in South Africa toward the end of the apartheid years, the lives of two incongruous people intersect, much like the two whose stories we have considered here. One is an elderly white woman, discouraged over the state of her country and fighting a losing battle with cancer. The other is a homeless black man with weathered skin and baggy pants, whom the woman discovers living in a cardboard box in the alley behind her house.

One afternoon, as she tries to hold back a wave of hopelessness, she sits down at the piano in her living room and plays some old pieces of music. She plays the notes "dryly and badly," searching for a chord that will comfort her. Finally, desperately, she turns to Bach. "The sounds that she makes are muddy, the lines are blurred, but every now and then the real thing emerges. The real music, the music that does not die, the music that is confident and serene. She plays the music for herself, but at one point, a shadow passes across the curtain, and she knows that the man who lives in the alley is listening outside, and so, she plays a bit of Bach for him, as well."[3]

Two people, their hearts "bound together" in a common hope for a different outcome from the one they expect. And here we are, bound together ourselves by a common hope, by a common search for the real thing, for a power that will make us whole.

May none leave here wanting. May that which is dead in you be raised up. May the power of God and the grace of our Lord Jesus Christ make that which is broken in you whole today.

NOTES

1. Walter Brueggemann et al. *Texts for Preaching, Year B* (Louisville, Ky.: Westminster John Knox Press, 1993).
2. *The Women's Bible Commentary*, ed. Carol A. Newsom and Sharon H. Ringe (Louisville, Ky.: Westminster John Knox Press, 1992), 268.
3. J. M. Coetzee, *Age of Iron* (New York: Random House, 1990), 24.

PART 2

Being a
Hospitable Church

Come as You Are

The Hospitable Church in the *Book of Confessions*

Ellen L. Babinsky

The *Book of Confessions* has a good deal to teach us about the immensity, the depth, and the mystery of God's grace extended toward all humanity in Jesus Christ. The tender regard of God for us as reflected in these texts is, in my view, the content and ground of the phrase "the hospitable church." We are able to declare the church to be hospitable to all God's people only as we are grasped by God's overwhelming, gracious hospitality to us in Jesus Christ.

In this essay I present my reflections about the nature of the hospitable church as I find it exhibited in the *Book of Confessions*. First, I ponder the true humanity of Jesus Christ as portrayed in the confessions, followed by my reflections on the inescapable human condition of sin. Next, I give consideration to a most difficult aspect of the confessions, namely, the doctrine of election, which, I argue, is crucial to our understanding of the hospitable church. Finally, I reflect on the hospitable church as the community of faith, by the power of the Holy Spirit made the body of Christ for the life of the world. I have been privileged and gratified by the insights I have gained in carrying out this task. I hope that what follows will be of service to my brothers and sisters in Christ and a praise to God.

Jesus Christ, Truly Human

The portrayal of Jesus Christ in the *Book of Confessions* is grounded in the classical terms of the Nicene and Apostles' Creeds, according to which Christ is declared to be truly divine and truly human. With a closer reading, however, I found that the texts demonstrate that Jesus Christ's true humanity consists of perfect relation with God, which is fulfillment of the law. The Heidelberg Catechism teaches that Jesus' great summary of the law in Matt. 22:37–40 shows us what is required to live the holy life: "You shall love the Lord your God with all your heart, and with all your soul, and with all your mind. . . . [Y]ou shall love your neighbor as yourself" (*BC* 4.004). In similar fashion, the Second Helvetic Confession declares that in the law we have been given the will of God:

> We teach that the will of God is explained for us in the law of God, what he wills or does not will us to do, what is good and just, or what is evil and unjust. Therefore, we confess that the law is good and holy. (*BC* 5.080)

When I say that Jesus Christ is truly human, then, I am saying that he fulfills the law utterly and completely, and therefore, in him all righteousness is fully revealed. To be truly human is to fulfill the law perfectly. When I read the confessions on the law in light of who Jesus Christ is, I am awestruck by his powerful and gracious hospitality toward all humanity, a theme to which I give more attention later in this essay.

This attention to the law also shows us the weakness of fallen humanity, our utter inability to fulfill the will of God, what we have become as a result of sin. The Heidelberg Catechism asks the penetrating question "Can you keep all this [that is, the law] perfectly?" to which the inescapable answer is "No, for by nature I am prone to hate God and my neighbor" (*BC* 4.005). The Confession of 1967 shows me how the presence of Christ reveals the darkness of our souls:

> The reconciling act of God in Jesus Christ exposes the evil in men as sin in the sight of God. In sin, men claim mastery of

their own lives, turn against God and their fellow men, and become exploiters and despoilers of the world. They lose their humanity in futile striving and are left in rebellion, despair, and isolation. (*BC* 9.12)

In this confession, as in the other confessions, no one escapes the judgment of God:

[A]ll human virtue, when seen in the light of God's love in Jesus Christ, is found to be infected by self-interest and hostility. All men, good and bad alike, are in the wrong before God and helpless without his forgiveness. Thus all men fall under God's judgment. No one is more subject to that judgment than the man who assumes that he is guiltless before God or morally superior to others. (*BC* 9.13)

The confessions teach, without equivocation, that a discussion of human merit is appropriate only in the context of God's judgment.

God's Elect in Christ

The mention of God's judgment turns my attention to the doctrine of predestination or election, which many persons find to be a most vexing doctrine. I find it necessary to ponder the doctrine of election, however, for two reasons. First, the doctrine of election appears in the *Book of Confessions*, and it seems arbitrary to summarily dismiss it, as if the doctrine had nothing to say to us in our time. Second, I believe the doctrine sheds light in an important way as I proceed in my reflection on the hospitable church. The doctrine is delineated most clearly in the Westminster Confession of Faith, although it appears in other confessions as well:

By the decree of God, for the manifestation of his glory, some men and angels are predestinated unto everlasting life, and others fore-ordained to everlasting death. (*BC* 6.016)

Those of mankind that are predestinated unto life, God, before the foundation of the world was laid, according to his eternal and immutable purpose, and the secret counsel and

good pleasure of his will, hath chosen in Christ, unto everlasting glory, out of his free grace and love alone, without any
foresight of faith or good works, or perseverance in either of
them, or any other thing in the creature, as conditions, or
causes moving him thereunto; and all to the praise of his
glorious grace. (*BC* 6.018)

Indeed, the doctrine seems utterly arbitrary in its declaration
of who is "in" and who is "out." What kind of hospitality summarily dismisses a portion of God's children, on what seems to
be nothing other than a whim that is monstrous in its implications? Why should a reflection on the hospitable church even
waste time on pondering such an odious way of thinking?

I offer some thoughts that I hope suggest ways in which to
construe the doctrine. The Second Helvetic Confession gives me
a helpful place to begin my reflection:

From eternity God has freely, and of his mere grace, without
any respect to men, predestinated or elected the saints whom
he wills to save in Christ. . . . (*BC* 5.052)
. . . Therefore, although not on account of any merit of
ours, God has elected us, not directly, but in Christ, and on
account of Christ, in order that those who are now ingrafted
into Christ by faith might also be elected. (*BC* 5.053)

Here I am instructed that Christ is the one in whom we are
saved according to the will of God, and on account of whom
believers are elected to salvation. Human merit is discounted.
This grace is a mystery for us because when we look at our own
reality, apart from God, there is nothing within us that could
account for God's overwhelming love for us. I emphasize here
the phrase "apart from God," for apart from God we would have
no existence at all; we would *be* nothing. The fact that I am able
to reflect on who I am, on my limitations and capacities, is, along
with all creation, a declaration of God's loving regard for me
before I ever came into this world. The doctrine of election
declares that in Christ we are made righteous for Christ's sake,
not because of who we are but because of who God is. The Second
Helvetic Confession gives me this word of encouragement:

Let Christ, therefore, be the looking glass, in whom we may contemplate our predestination. We shall have a sufficiently clear and sure testimony that we are inscribed in the Book of Life if we have fellowship with Christ, and he is ours and we are his in true faith. (*BC* 5.060)

The imagery is compelling: if Christ is my looking glass, then, when I look in this mirror, I see him, and not just him but I see myself in him. All that I am, all that I have done and will do, all that I possess, all is taken up into Christ, restored and made whole on account of the tender regard of God in Christ. I am not to look at myself, my deeds, my thoughts, my hopes, my dreams, or anything else about me in an attempt to figure out if I am among the elect. I am to look to Christ alone.

Moreover, the Second Helvetic Confession teaches me that any attempt on my part to discern whether or not I or anyone else might be of the elect is idle speculation that cannot be fruitfully undertaken:

And when the Lord was asked whether there were few that should be saved, he does not answer and tell them that few or many should be saved or damned, but rather he exhorts every man to "strive to enter by the narrow door" (Luke 13:24): as if he should say, It is not for you curiously to inquire about these matters, but rather to endeavor that you may enter into heaven by the straight way. (*BC* 5.056)

The question of who is saved is not ours to answer. The confessions teach that the doctrine of election means that we cannot know the status of anyone before God. An overzealous regard about our election or the election of anyone else distracts us from what *is* our concern, namely, love for God and neighbor, care for God's world and God's children, and ongoing humility required in the walk of faith.

The Gracious Hospitality of Jesus Christ

The teachings about election found in the confessions help me understand that there is absolutely nothing I can do to earn or

merit the promises of God in Jesus Christ. Indeed, if a discussion
of human merit is appropriate only in the context of divine judgment, the doctrine of election also teaches me that a discussion
of human sin is appropriate only in the context of the gracious
hospitality of God in Jesus Christ. I am utterly helpless, completely unable on my own to will the goodness, to choose the
goodness, that is God's will. I cannot come to Jesus Christ to
receive these promises by my own wisdom and insight. Rather,
the very yearning I have for the presence of God is the work of
the Holy Spirit, who is one with the Father and with the Son.
The Scots Confession in particular instructs me that our capacities for choosing God's ways are the gift of God alone, without
any merit on our part:

> [A]s we confess that God the Father created us when we
> were not, as his Son our Lord Jesus redeemed us when we
> were enemies to him, so also do we confess that the Holy
> Ghost does sanctify and regenerate us, without respect to any
> merit proceeding from us, be it before or be it after our
> regeneration. To put this even more plainly; as we willingly
> disclaim any honor and glory for our own creation and
> redemption, so do we willingly also for our regeneration and
> sanctification; for by ourselves we are not capable of thinking
> one good thought, but he who has begun the work in us alone
> continues us in it, to the praise and glory of his undeserved
> grace. (*BC* 3.12)

I cannot overstate how crucial this declaration is to my understanding of the doctrine of election. God brought me into this
world. I was redeemed by God in Jesus Christ while I was alien-
ated from God and neighbor. I am made willing to desire to be
a loving neighbor by God, through the work and power of the
Holy Spirit. Am I able to pray? Thanks be to God. Am I able to
extend a helping hand in some way? Thanks be to God. Has
some event or series of events led me into an ever-deepening
trust in God? Thanks be to God in Christ, whose loving-kindness
never ends and never fails. I am able to grow in faithfulness
because in Jesus Christ I am promised that God is ever faithful to
me in all ways, beyond my knowing.

Jesus Christ, Our Hope

Reflecting on the doctrine of election, then, I find a deep freedom from which flows a strong hope. If God is the one who sustains and guides me in Christ through the power of the Holy Spirit, what or whom should I fear? The Westminster Confession of Faith declares with ringing clarity the foundation of this freedom and hope:

> God alone is Lord of the conscience, and hath left it free from the doctrines and commandments of men which are in anything contrary to his Word, or beside it in matters of faith or worship. So that to believe such doctrines, or to obey such commandments out of conscience, is to betray true liberty of conscience; and the requiring an implicit faith, and an absolute and blind obedience, is to destroy liberty of conscience, and reason also. (*BC* 6.109)

To say "God alone is Lord of the conscience" does not mean that I am thereby licensed to do whatever I want. *God* is Lord of my conscience, not my culture, my job, my nation, or anything else I might dream up as a way to hide from God's claim on me, which is God's law. When I ponder what is taught about the law in the confessions, I am made aware that I cannot fulfill what the law requires.

For instance, the Heidelberg Catechism instructs me that in the Eighth Commandment ("you shall not steal"), God requires:

> That I work for the good of my neighbor wherever I can and may, deal with him as I would have others deal with me, and do my work well so that I may be able to help the poor in their need. (*BC* 4.111)

While I could confidently declare that I have never stolen from anyone, I cannot claim that "I work for the good of my neighbor wherever I can and may." I certainly cannot claim that "I do my work well so that I may be able to help the poor in their need." I cannot, of my own strength of will and inclination, fulfill what is required in the law. God's law convicts me and teaches me to turn to Christ, to find my hope of justification in him alone. According to the Second Helvetic Confession, the law is given "that . . . from what it teaches we may know (our) weakness, sin and condemnation, and, despairing of our strength, might be converted to Christ in faith" (*BC* 5.083). We have no recourse except to cling to Jesus Christ, who covers us with his righteousness, as the Scots Confession declares:

> For as God the Father beholds us in the body of his Son Christ Jesus, he accepts our imperfect obedience as if it were perfect, and covers our works, which are defiled with many stains, with the righteousness of his Son. We do not mean that we are so set at liberty that we owe no obedience to the Law . . . but we affirm that no man on earth, with the sole exception of Christ Jesus, has given, gives, or shall give in action that obedience to the Law which the Law requires. (*BC* 3.15)

Nevertheless, since God is Lord of my conscience, I therefore must pray for God's help. But even here, the deep struggle is to have the courage to pray the Holy Spirit to give me the willingness to desire to "work for the good of my neighbor" and "do my work well so that I may be able to help the poor in their need."

What I mean by a deep freedom and a deep hope, then, is that in Christ I am made free to grow in faithfulness. In Christ I am given hope in the promises of God that I will be sustained in my desire to grow in faithfulness. The context for my growing in faithfulness is the church, the community of those who acknowledge the claim of God in Christ as Lord of their lives and consciences. As a company of believers, we stake our lives on and rejoice in the hospitality of Jesus Christ. Together we work and pray that the church on earth might reflect this hospitality as the body of Christ for the life of the world.

The Hospitable Church

As Jesus Christ extends his gracious hospitality to all who turn to him, so also the hospitable church, the body of Christ, extends the gracious hospitality of Christ to all who come to receive the promises of God. The Second Helvetic Confession is particularly clear that the church belongs to Christ and not to us. This confession declares that those who separate themselves from the fellowship of the true church of God cannot hope to stand before God. Nevertheless, this confession also makes clear that we on earth can in no way determine who might be included in or separated from the true church of God.

> Nevertheless, . . . we do not so narrowly restrict the Church as to teach that all those are outside the Church who either do not participate in the Sacraments, at least not willingly and through contempt, but rather, being forced by necessity, unwillingly abstain from them or are deprived of them; or in whom faith sometimes fails, though it is not entirely extinguished and does not wholly cease; or in whom imperfections and errors due to weakness are found. . . . We know what happened to St. Peter, who denied his Master, and what is wont to happen daily to God's elect and faithful people who go astray and are weak. We know, moreover, what kind of churches the churches in Galatia and Corinth were in the apostles' time, in which the apostle found fault with many serious offenses; yet he calls them holy churches of Christ. (BC 5.137)

Here we are instructed by the Second Helvetic Confession that there may be some who seem to be separated from the visible church as we know it yet who remain counted among the faithful in God's eyes. Likewise, this confession reminds us that we are not to assume that all persons active in the church are to be numbered among the members of the true church of God:

> Again, not all that are reckoned in the number of the Church are saints, and living and true members of the Church. For there are many hypocrites, who outwardly hear the Word of God, and publicly receive the Sacraments, and seem to pray to God through Christ alone, to confess Christ to be their only righteousness, and to worship God, and to exercise the duties of charity, and for a time to endure with patience in misfortune. And yet they are inwardly destitute of true illumination of the Spirit, of faith and sincerity of heart, and of

perseverance to the end. But eventually the character of these men, for the most part, will be disclosed. . . . And although while they simulate piety they are not of the Church, yet they are considered to be in the Church. . . . And therefore the Church of God is rightly compared to a net which catches fish of all kinds, and to a field, in which both wheat and tares are found. (*BC* 5.139)

These instructions from the Second Helvetic Confession are clearly grounded in the doctrine of election. We cannot know with certainty in this life who is the true member of the true church of God, because it is not given to us to know who among us are the elect of God. The confession continues that since we cannot know the identity of the true member of the true church, we must take extraordinary care how we set the boundaries of the church:

Hence we must be very careful not to judge before the time, nor undertake to exclude, reject or cut off those whom the Lord does not want to have excluded or rejected, and those whom we cannot eliminate without loss to the Church. On the other hand, we must be vigilant lest while the pious snore the wicked gain ground and do harm to the Church. (*BC* 5.140)

Jesus Christ is the true guardian of his church. At the same time, while we cannot know with certainty who are the true members, we still have the obligation to be thoughtful, observant, and engaged members of the community of faith. That we cannot know with certainty need not reduce us to a passive apathy about the ministry and mission of the church. On the contrary, we are to engage one another with sincerity, charity, and humility with regard to the proclamation of the gospel and the promises of God in Jesus Christ to all people. Controversies and divisions are perhaps better understood as the grappling of those who seek to be faithful followers of Jesus of Nazareth in all its implications for life together in Christian community. Disagreements in the church are best seen as sincere and differing quests for the truth in Jesus Christ. Humility is the most helpful response in divisive times. Participants in such disputes who see themselves as the sole possessors of the truth dishonor the portion of the truth they do possess and disregard (to their peril) the humility to which Christ calls us as we grow in faithfulness.

We do well to listen to ourselves and to one another when we speak of unity, for all too frequently the term *unity* masks a hidden desire for *uniformity*. At the same time, we cannot simply lift up diversity as a positive value in the name of "unity," in an effort to avoid tensions and conflicts. I believe that we can claim the essential marks of our faith as binding while affirming a diversity that need not divide. Here the Second Helvetic Confession points a way for us, but it is a path that is nonetheless not easily discerned:

> Furthermore, we diligently teach that care is to be taken wherein the truth and unity of the Church chiefly lies, lest we rashly provoke and foster schisms in the Church. Unity consists not in outward rites and ceremonies, but rather in the truth and unity of the catholic faith. The catholic faith is not given to us by human laws, but by Holy Scriptures, of which the Apostles' Creed is a compendium. And, therefore, we read in the ancient writers that there was a manifold diversity of rites, but that they were free, and no one ever thought that the unity of the Church was thereby dissolved. So we teach that the true harmony of the Church consists in doctrines and in the true and harmonious preaching of the Gospel of Christ, and in rites that have been expressly delivered by the Lord. (*BC* 5.141)

The difficulty, of course, lies in the task of discerning what the essential tenets of Christian faith are for our time. Would ordination to offices of leadership of persons who are gay, lesbian, transgendered, or bisexual signal deep schism, an abandonment of true doctrine? Or would such ordinations be viewed as a difference of practice that is embraced by an overarching unity? I believe the latter alternative to be the way more true to the gospel promises of Jesus Christ. Because I trust in God who calls us to faith, who calls us to trust in the divine promises of grace in Jesus Christ, I therefore trust that God will guide us toward the divine and prophetic vision of the peaceable kingdom. If I err, I desire to err on the side of God's grace extended in the gracious hospitality of Jesus Christ to all people as I pray to be obedient to Jesus Christ, under the authority of scriptures and guided by the confessions.

The Church
and God's Pentecostal Gift

Letty M. Russell

When I was a pastor in the Presbyterian Church of the Ascension in the East Harlem Protestant Parish, we served a low-income community that was multilingual, multiracial, and multiethnic. Our worship services were a little like Pentecost, with the use of Spanish and English and a slightly chaotic atmosphere of welcome to people regardless of age, economic status, or attire. The services shared the Reformed tradition in various languages and cultures so that it spoke of justice and new life. To express unity in Christ, we placed the pews around the communion table so that we could be one community breaking bread and sharing the word.

One Pentecost, the children made beautiful white doves out of helium balloons. A number of these found their way up to the ceiling of the sanctuary as we gathered in church. Just as we stood around the table and shared the blessing of the bread and wine, one of these doves settled gently on the loaf of bread! The children's gift had renewed our vision of the Spirit who makes us one.

The symbol of the dove used in Matthew's story of Jesus' baptism and the symbol of fire used in Luke's story of the birth of the church continue to remind us of the presence of God's love among us and of our calling to join as one people to serve others

51

in Christ's name (Matt. 3:16; Acts 2:3). This calling is spelled out for us in the Presbyterian *Book of Order* by a description of the six great ends of the church (G-1.0200): proclaiming the gospel, nurturing the children of God, maintaining divine worship, preserving the truth of the gospel, promoting social righteousness, and exhibiting the kingdom of heaven to the world. These great ends were symbolized by six banners at the 1999 General Assembly, with a dove representing God's Pentecostal gift of the Holy Spirit woven into the tapestry of each banner, symbolizing the presence of Christ's Spirit among us, nurturing the church and helping us draw near to God and to one another.[1] As John Calvin puts it:

> God has, in [God's] wonderful providence, accommodated [God's self] to our capacity, by prescribing [in the church] a way for us in which we might approach [God], notwithstanding our immense distance from [God].[2]

It is in the power of the Holy Spirit that the church is enabled to serve the great ends and participate in God's intention to reconcile the world and to mend the creation.

As we seek to renew our vision of Reformed faith and life in the church for the twenty-first century, our experiences of the Spirit in our lives call us to look carefully at the tradition of Pentecost and the gift of the Spirit in order to see if our study of scriptures might point us toward a new vision of unity in the midst of the ever-increasing diversity of our churches. In this essay, I suggest that this new vision leads to a different understanding of unity and of the church, an understanding based in the practice of God's hospitality.

God's Pentecostal Gift

At the luncheon I attended recently, Peter Gomes, chaplain at Harvard University, gave a lecture that provides us with another way of looking at the story of Pentecost. Gomes said that the important part of the Spirit's work at Pentecost was not so much the ecstasy of the moment but the *Spirit-induced understanding:*

That was the thing that the Spirit did, and that was how the people could say that they each heard in their own language the wonderful works of God. The work of the Spirit is designed to foster understanding and ultimate reconciliation.[3]

To understand why God's Pentecostal gift of understanding is so important, we need to go back and look at the text and to the story of the tower of Babel, which tells of the advent of misunderstanding at the dawn of human history.

Babel's Gift

The story of the tower of Babel in Gen. 11:1–9 is part of the prologue to the call of Abraham and Sarah in chapter 12 and the beginning of the story of God's desire to be in covenant relationship with women and men and with all creation. This prologue describes the way in which the authors experience alienation and sin in their world: human sin (chap. 3), spiritual sin (chap. 6), and social-structural sin (chap. 11).[4] Like the other accounts, this fall of the nations, with the resulting confusion of their language and dispersal across the earth, points toward God's actions to limit the results of sin.

In the Babel story, the scattering and the confusion of language are God's response to those who seek to triumph through domination. By building the tower to heaven, these people tried to consolidate their power and to become like God, controlling all the people through a unified language and political structure. Even the name, Babel, evokes in the hearers' minds the dominating power of the Babylonian empire and the intention of unity without diversity.

God's response is the *gift of diversity*. According to José Míguez-Bonino, God's action is twofold:

the thwarting of the project of the false unity of domination *and* the liberation of the nations that possess their own races, languages, and families.[5]

One cannot solve problems of difference by simply eliminating them through the imposition of one dominant pattern.

Differences of race, gender, sexual orientation, language, and culture are not problems to be solved and controlled by a dominant group but rather important ways of assuring that God's gift of diversity in all creation will continue. Because of God's gift, new voices can be heard and languages and cultures can flourish. Such a message is doubly important for us today as we watch the growing domination of the world by one economic system and the growing requirement that people learn English in order to be included in its global economic outreach.

Pentecost's Gift

The story of Pentecost in Acts 2:1–21 has often been understood as a sign of the reversal of Babel, as nations are brought together and united in the outpouring of Christ's Spirit and the birth of the church. But we need to look again at its message of unity, in the light of our understanding that God's gift at Babel was one of diversity. If diversity is a gift, surely it is not something to be overcome, any more than we would want to overcome God's gift of unity in Christ.

One way to look at this would be to use the clue from Peter Gomes that Pentecost is about the *gift of understanding.* God makes unity possible by the gift of the Spirit, which enables people of all nations to understand one another, no matter what language is spoken. Acts 2:6 says that "each one heard them speaking in the native language of each."[6] It does not say that they no longer had their own languages and customs but rather that they could understand one another. This is a different kind of unity than the one envisioned by the builders at Babel. Here the unity comes not through domination or uniformity but through communication.

God's inclusive Spirit not only makes it possible to understand one another in the Spirit but also makes it possible for *many voices to be heard* and included in the center of the discussion.[7] The structures of domination are challenged as women prophesy together with men and as slaves and those at the margins of society receive the Spirit (Acts 2:17–18). The church is born as a community of equals, whose unity comes through the love of Christ and is proclaimed and lived out in many and diverse ways (Acts 2:43–47). The gift of unity is not separate from diversity but rather an expression of community, as people are called to share their many gifts. We discover, as Audre Lorde has put it, that there are real differences among us of race, age, gender, and orientation, and that these are gifts not problems.

> [I]t is not those differences between us that are separating us. It is rather *our refusal to recognize those differences*, and to examine the distortions which result from our misnaming them and their effects upon human behavior and expectation.[8]

God's Pentecostal gift of understanding in diversity pushes us toward a unity that is based on our ability to welcome all people and to include their voices in the life of the church.

A Different Kind of Unity

Our clues from the study of Babel and Pentecost lead us to expect that God has a different kind of unity from that which we try to establish through revisions of our form of government, such as "Amendment B" of the *Book of Order*, designed to tighten uniformity in the requirements for ordination (G-6.0106b).[9] José Míguez-Bonino puts the question to us this way:

> God re-creates the diversity that some want to homogenize. For this reason, God must constantly "scatter the proud in the imaginations of their hearts" [Luke 1:51], so that the humble may live in freedom. The question that remains for us is whether there *is a different kind of unity*, a different universality, that does not rest in the elimination of all languages, the centralization of all locality, the submission of one city, or the worshiping of one tower.[10]

We already have some clues to what this different unity might look like, but here I first expand the scriptural clues about diversity and understanding by looking at the basic paradigm shift in how we understand the world and the church that is necessary if we are to envision this new unity and seek to live it out in our churches.

Unity-in-Tension

One paradigm or view of reality and how we live in our world is to see unity always in tension with diversity. As Jack Stotts, president emeritus of Austin Presbyterian Theological Seminary, has said:

> Individually and together we reside in the tension between what James Luther Adams calls opposing virtues—the virtue of unity and the virtue of diversity.[11]

This paradigm emerged out of discussions in the ecumenical movement, as churches in the World Council of Churches (WCC) and other bilateral conversations began to focus on ways in which "all may be one" in Jesus Christ yet manifest that oneness in and through different understandings of faith and order in different confessional families (John 17:21).

As we moved toward the end of the twentieth century, it became clear that the global diversity of churches, as well as the diversity among churches in one region, no longer allowed the ecumenical movement to speak only of "ecclesiastical unity" that could be achieved in the churches through common confession of apostolic faith; mutual recognition of baptism, Eucharist, and ministry; and common ways of making decisions and teaching authoritatively.[12]

By the time of the Fifth Assembly of the WCC in Nairobi in 1975, the churches had begun to speak of "unity-in-tension" and to recognize the connection of church unity and community to issues of justice and reconciliation.[13] It was still possible to share in the faith that we are made one in Jesus Christ but no longer possible to imagine that this unity could be established in the churches without new attention to the issues of justice in our world. The "great end of the church" concerned with social righteousness became an important part of unity as the churches recognized the changing agenda of the twenty-first century, where unity and diversity are no longer workable as a metaphors for pluralistic communities in which all persons are seeking for a voice and a chance to be heard in their own language of faith.

The paradigm of unity-in-tension no longer works because we can no longer achieve unity by *limiting diversity*.[14] Diversity itself is a major factor in world reality and has become one of the key elements of resistance to global capitalism and economic, political, and cultural uniformity. This older paradigm is based on structures of domination and on dualistic thinking. It still serves those who wish to accumulate power over others and to win unity by the loss of the dignity and full humanity of others. But it does not serve a desire for unity in Christ in which persons are welcomed and understood in their own languages, cultures, and lifestyles. Its dualistic way of thinking always assumes that we can have unity *or* diversity, and that unity is achieved by limiting or co-opting or destroying difference.

Instead of trying to hold things in tension as the differences increase, we need to turn to scripture to look for other metaphors of unity in Christ. As Thomas Best has said, we need to "move beyond unity-in-tension toward a vision of more complete community."[15] This would be a vision that lifts up Paul's emphasis on the unity of the resurrected body of Christ and the variety of gifts of the Spirit (1 Corinthians 12). It would be a vision that includes women and men, slave and free, Jew and Greek, gay and straight, young and old, persons with disabilities and abilities, rich and poor, and so many more as those who speak in the power of the Holy Spirit (Acts 2:6; Gal. 3:28).

Unity in Hospitality

One possible way of describing a paradigm of a different kind of unity is to begin with God's concern to welcome all persons and to speak of unity in hospitality. Hospitality is an expression of unity without uniformity. Through hospitality, community is built out of difference, not sameness. In this way of thinking there is no "either-or," "right-wrong," "win-lose." Rather, there are many possible options for faithful expression of our unity in

Christ. Hospitality in community is a sharing of the openness of Christ to all as he welcomed them into God's kingdom. Because unity in Christ has as its purpose the sharing of God's hospitality with the stranger, the one who is "other," it assumes that unity and diversity belong together.[16] When they are not together, and unity is achieved through exclusion or domination of those who are different, this is no longer unity in Christ.

The Greek New Testament abounds in exhortations to hospitality. John Koenig says in *New Testament Hospitality* that

> *philoxenia*, the term for hospitality used in the New Testament, refers literally not to a love of strangers *per se* but to a delight in the whole guest-host relationship, in the mysterious reversals and gains for all parties which may take place. For believers, this delight is fueled by the expectation that God or Christ or the Holy Spirit will play a role in every hospitable transaction [Heb. 13:2; Rom. 1.11–12].[17]

Koenig describes hospitality as "partnership with strangers" and understands hospitality as "the catalyst for creating and sustaining partnerships in the gospel."[18] The Greek word *philoxenia* means "love of the stranger." It is the opposite of *xenophobia*, which means "hatred of the stranger" or of the one who is different. We are exhorted to hospitality by Paul, who bids us "welcome one another" as Christ has welcomed us (Rom. 15:7).

The "Call to Covenant Community" of the Covenant Network of Presbyterians also exhorts us to hospitality:

> The church we seek to strengthen is built upon the hospitality of Jesus, who said, "Whoever comes to me I will not cast out." The good news of the gospel is that all—those who are near and those who were far off—are invited; all are members of the household and citizens of the realm of God. No one has a claim on this invitation and none of us becomes worthy, even by sincere effort to live according to God's will. Grateful for our own inclusion, we carry out the mission of the church to extend God's hospitality to a broken and fearful and lonely world.[19]

Many groups in the Presbyterian Church would agree to this call for hospitality, and it provides a clue to the possibility of wel-

coming diversity rather than creating an "easy unity" built on
compliance with one interpretation of faith in Christ. For
instance, Presbyterian Promise, a group in formation in the
Presbytery of Southern New England, has this mission statement:

> To proclaim God's promise of justice and love in Jesus Christ
> by organizing inclusive and inquiring churches in the
> Presbytery of Southern New England into a community of
> mutual support for the empowerment of Gay, Lesbian,
> Bisexual, and Transgendered persons, and for outreach, edu-
> cation, and Christian evangelism.[20]

This group seeks to reach out in evangelism and welcome to
persons who have been excluded from the hospitality of the
church because of their sexual orientation. At the same time, it
seeks to evangelize congregations so that they become less fearful of difference and more open to welcoming others as Christ
has welcomed them. Understanding unity in a paradigm of hospitality will not take away all the tension, disagreement, and pain
over ordination of gay, lesbian, bisexual, and transgendered persons, but it may lead us to accept one another in our differences
and to focus on the tasks of service and mission that we can do
together. [21]

When we welcome those who come from different contexts
and life experiences, we learn from them, and we learn that
there are many ways in which to understand and live out our
unity in Christ. These different ways can also open up our
churches as we seek to become partners with those who are different by sharing together in mission and service to others. In
this way we leave off building our institutional "towers" and
begin to focus on mutual understanding and our calling to serve
in the world.

A Different Kind of Church

If a paradigm shift to hospitality can lead to a different kind of
unity, then how will this shift lead to a different understanding

of the church? If we are able to move together as a denomination and find a way to welcome difference and seek understanding through the Spirit, the Presbyterian Church (U.S.A.) will in some respects become a different kind of church.[22] Many local congregations have already led the way as they have worked together to reach out to those in their communities regardless of race, class, gender, ability, or sexual orientation. One church I worked with recently showed outstanding concern to listen to all perspectives in the discussion of ways to include gay and lesbian persons in the life of their church. For example, the church held a series of meetings to explore the meaning of covenant relationships through discussion of biblical and theological perspectives as well as through presentations by couples who were in many different relationships and lifestyles. The atmosphere of hospitality and seeking to learn from one another was a way to practice the presence of God's Spirit of understanding.

Community of Christ

Looked at from the perspective of hospitality, the church could be understood as "a community of Christ, bought with a price, where everyone is welcome."[23] It is a *community of Christ* because Christ's presence, through the power of the Spirit, constitutes people as a community gathered in Christ's name (Matt. 18:20; 1 Cor. 12:4–6). This community is *bought with a price* because the struggle of Jesus to overcome the structures of sin and death constitutes both the source of new life in the community and its own mandate to continue the same struggle for life on behalf of others (1 Cor. 6:20; Phil. 2:1–11). It is a community *where everyone is welcome* because it gathers around the table of God's hospitality. Its welcome table is a sign of the coming feast of God's mended creation, with the guest list derived from the announcements of the jubilee year and of Pentecostal gifts of understanding and inclusion (Luke 14:12–14; Acts 2:1–21).

In his book *The Church in the Power of the Spirit*, Jürgen Moltmann speaks of three promises of Christ's presence among us.[24] The first set of promises constitutes those of presence in the gospel, in word and sacrament, and in the gathered community (Matt. 28:18–20; 1 Cor. 11:23–26; Matt. 18:20). The second set of promises is related to the poor and marginalized (Matt. 25:31–46). The third set is related to Christ's future coming and the mending of creation (Matt. 25:31–46). Christ promises to be present wherever God's will for love, justice, and peace is done on earth as in heaven (Matt. 6:10). Moltmann underlines this justice connection, saying that

> the one who is to come is then already present in an anticipatory sense in history in the Spirit and the word, and in the miserable and helpless. His future ends the world's history of suffering and completes the fragments and anticipations of his kingdom which are called the church.[25]

The Unity We Seek

In this understanding of church as community of Christ where everyone is welcome, the source of unity is the gift of Christ's presence in our midst, calling us to be open to others. The test of that unity is how well our churches break down barriers and welcome those who have been at the margins of church and society (Luke 4:18–19). One way in which the church has been tested in its hospitality over the last forty years has been through the push for full inclusion and partnership in the life of the church by women of all colors. Women are now able to participate fully as pastors, elders, and deacons, yet they often find themselves limited and marginalized in the decision making of the church. For instance, the attempt to control the church has often focused on limiting the prophetic role of women, as in the case of the controversy over the Re-Imagining Conference as well as in the current controversies at the 1999 General Assembly over the National Network of Presbyterian College Women, Review of the Women's Ministries, and the Women of Faith Awards by Women's Ministries.[26] In each case, no matter what the particular issue, the response of the church has been to limit and restrict the women theologically, financially, and programmatically. In the old unity-in-tension power struggles, the women are used as pawns whose dignity and participation in the church is simply a problem.

If we spend our time erecting barriers against those who are considered marginal because of class, race, sexual orientation, or gender, we have moved away from the paradigm of hospitality. If, by contrast, we struggle for ways in which to work through our differences without demeaning those we consider unimportant, we can move toward a unity based on hospitality. Unity in this different kind of church would include many perspectives and would come out of much struggle and pain. Yet we can suggest a few clues to what that unity would look like for a church of hospitality.

The first clue would be that in Christ, *unity is a given*. As did our foremothers and forefathers, we understand that unity is a gift of God and that our calling is to live out that gift. In Christ, God has made us one and given us the witness of the Holy Spirit to guide and nurture us, so that we might become a community of understanding even in the midst of our alienation. At Pentecost this unity was confirmed by the offer of baptism into Christ and the reception of the Holy Spirit when "about three thousand persons were added" (Acts 2:42).

The second clue is that in Christ, *difference is a given*. God intends for many voices, cultures, and languages and presses the church to be part of every nation and culture, growing and learning from the differences of people in its midst and in the world around it. Dealing with difference in the church does not require limitations but only the willingness to listen and learn together and to find the ways to common service in the name of Christ. One witness of Babel is that difference is God's gift, which makes possible the riotous diversity of our world.

The third clue is that in Christ, *hospitality is a given*. By his parables of God's kingdom, Jesus reminds us over and over that God welcomes all those who have been marginal to religious and social institutions. Practicing hospitality by seeking justice, peace, and wholeness for all persons and for all creation is a way of living out our faith in Jesus Christ. The Pentecostal gift of understanding makes possible hospitality among persons of great diversity as they listen to one another and learn together about the ways of the Spirit in their lives and communities.

The final clue is that in Christ, *unity is an impossible possibility*. Although the church is one in Christ, it lives each day torn by difference and seeking to manifest that oneness. It lives each day with the impossible possibility that one day God will fulfill the unity of the church and mend the creation that has been so torn apart. Then each of us will cease to live *apart* from others and become *a part* of God's beautifully diverse creation. At moments when this unity happens among people, it is so surprising that the people are amazed and think, like some of the crowd at Pentecost, that "[t]hey are filled with new wine" (Acts 2:13).

As we search for the unity that has been given to us in Jesus Christ, we are guided in the church by the gift of the Holy Spirit. This is symbolized on the seal of the Presbyterian Church (U.S.A.) as a dove, descending over the cross and open book to inspire us with God's love that opens us to others. The cross itself is open on the sides, stretching out and inviting us to reach toward the rainbow of diversity that is so much a part of our faith and life in the twenty-first century.

On either side of the cross, the seal also has the Spirit presented as flames of fire. The Spirit is descending on the church as tongues of flame, inspiring understanding among all God's people. It is present to the church as a burning bush that is not quenched, witnessing to God's power in the midst of struggle and suffering. It moves ahead of the church as a pillar of fire to guide it and renew its vision for the future.

NOTES

1. The banners used at the 211th General Assembly were created by Annadell Teems, member of the Committee on Local Arrangements of Grace Presbytery. They will be given to Columbia Theological Seminary in honor of Douglas Oldenburg, Moderator of the 210th General Assembly (1998).
2. John Calvin, *Institutes of the Christian Religion*, trans. John Allen, 7th ed. (Philadelphia: Board of Christian Education, 1936), IV, 1, 1, pp. 269–70. See "The Church," in *Feminist Theory and*

64   Letty M. Russell

Theology, by Serene Jones (Minneapolis: Fortress Press, forth-coming).

3. Peter Gomes, "Beyond the Human Point of View." Available at http://www.covenantnetwork.org/gomes.html or from the Covenant Network Administrative Office, c/o Calvary Presbyterian Church, 2515 Fillmore St., San Francisco, CA 94115.

4. Walter Wink, *Engaging the Powers: Discernment and Resistance in a World of Domination* (Minneapolis: Fortress Press, 1992), 77.

5. José Míguez-Bonino, "Genesis 11:1–9: A Latin American Perspective," in *Return to Babel: Global Perspectives on the Bible*, ed. Priscilla Pope-Levison and John R. Levison (Louisville, Ky.: Westminster John Knox Press, 1999), 15.

6. Unless otherwise indicated, scripture quotations are from the New Revised Standard Version of the Bible, copyright © 1989 by the Division of Christian Education of the National Council of the Churches of Christ in the U.S.A.

7. Justo L. González, "Reading from My Bicultural Place," in *Reading from This Place: Social Location and Biblical Interpretation in the United States*, ed. Fernando F. Segovia and Mary Ann Tolbert (Minneapolis: Fortress Press, 1995), 1:146–47.

8. Andre Lorde, *Sister Outsider: Essays and Speeches* (Trumansburg, N.Y.: Crossing Press, 1984), 115.

9. For discussion of Amendment B and the issues surrounding it, see "Session Four: Unity in Diversity," in *A Call to Covenant Community Study Guide*, by Erwin C. Barron (San Francisco: Covenant Network of Presbyterians, 1999), 21–26.

10. Míguez-Bonino, "Genesis 11:1–9," 16.

11. Jack Stotts, "Unity and Diversity: An Enduring Agenda." Available at http://www.covenantnetwork.org/stottstalk.html or from the Covenant Network Administrative Office, c/o Calvary Presbyterian Church, 2515 Fillmore Street, San Francisco, CA 94115.

12. Mary Ann Lundy, "Unity and Diversity," in *Dictionary of Feminist Theologies*, ed. Letty M. Russell and J. Shannon Clarkson (Louisville, Ky.: Westminster John Knox Press, 1996), 305–6.

13. Thomas F. Best, ed., *Beyond Unity-in-Tension*, Faith and Order Paper no. 138 (Geneva: WCC Publications, 1988), 1, 22.

14. Michael Kinnamon, *Truth and Community: Diversity and Its Limits in the Ecumenical Movement* (Grand Rapids: Wm. B. Eerdmans Publishing Co., 1988), 1–18.

15. Best, ed., *Beyond Unity-in-Tension*, 27.

16. See Letty M. Russell, *Church in the Round: Feminist Interpretation of the Church* (Louisville, Ky.: Westminster/John Knox Press, 1993), 172–175.

17. John Koenig, *New Testament Hospitality: Partnership with Strangers as Promise and Mission* (Philadelphia: Fortress Press, 1985), 8.
18. Ibid., 10; Russell, *Church in the Round*, 173.
19. "A Call to Covenant Community," 1997. Copies available from the Covenant Network Administrative Office, c/o Calvary Presbyterian Church, 2515 Fillmore St., San Francisco, CA 94115, or http://www.covenantnetwork.org. See Appendix.
20. Minutes of the More Light Presbyterians of the Presbytery of Southern New England, July 3, 1999.
21. Minority Report on the overture of Milwaukee Presbytery on striking G-6.0106b from the *Book of Order*, 211th General Assembly (1999).
22. Joseph D. Small, "Signs of the Post-Denominational Future," *Christian Century* 116, no. 14 (May 5, 1999): 506–9.
23. Russell, *Church in the Round*, 14.
24. Jürgen Moltmann, *The Church in the Power of the Spirit: A Contribution to Messianic Ecclesiology* (San Francisco: Harper & Row, 1977), 121–32.
25. Ibid., 132.
26. Doug King, "Presbyterian Women Assert the Freedom to Choose . . . Who Will Get Awards," *Network News* (The Witherspoon Society), 19, no. 2 (spring 1999): 7.

The Church That Is Alive Is Loyal to the Past but Open to the Future

1 Thessalonians 5:19–22

Robert Bohl

The church that is alive is loyal to the past but open to the future! If you take a serious analytical look at the history of the Christian church from its beginning, with the twelve Jesus chose, right down to this very moment, to you and me, the miracle is not so much in the fact that the church has survived. The miracle is in the fact that God has done so many incredibly great things through us. And those great things have been done in spite of our quirks, our broken promises, our controversies, our heated arguments, our positions of theological arrogance, our criticisms of one another.

W. C. Fields, no paragon of virtue, once observed, with a twinkle in his eyes: "Wouldn't it be terrible if I quoted some reliable statistics which prove that more people are driven to do insane things through religious hysteria than by drinking alcohol!" He declared, "A fanatic with a Bible can be more dangerous than a fanatic with a bottle!" Quibble with that if you will, but don't miss its implied truth. Suppose for a moment you were Jesus and you had reached the point where it was time to leave the carpenter shop and begin your public ministry. Suppose you were Jesus and you decided to choose twelve to be a part of your core organization. Where would you begin? What criteria would you establish? What moral and theological parameters would you employ? Just how much would you leave to God to influence you?

Today we probably would employ a professional search corporation for personnel and all sorts of consultants. Then suppose you were Jesus and you submitted twelve names for the consultant to evaluate. It seems their evaluation might come back in this kind of report:

> *Dear Jesus:*
> *Thank you for submitting the résumés of the twelve you have picked for management positions in your new organization. All of them have taken our battery of tests and have had personal interviews with our psychologist. We do not believe any of them has a team spirit, and we would recommend you continue your search for persons of experience in management and for persons of proven ability.*
> *Simon Peter is emotionally unstable and given to fits of temper. Andrew has absolutely no leadership ability. The two brothers, James and John, place personal ambitions above company loyalty. Thomas's questioning attitude would tend to undermine morale. We feel it is our duty to inform you that Matthew has been bad-listed by the Greater Jerusalem Better Business Bureau. James, the son of Alphaeus, definitely has radical leanings.*
> *One of the candidates, however, shows great potential. He is a man of ability and resourcefulness, has a keen business mind, and has contacts in high places. He is highly motivated, ambitious, and respectable. We recommend Judas Iscariot as your controller and most trusted leader. We further recommend that you seek eleven others who are more qualified than those you first submitted.*

That is a startling reminder that Jesus is always surprising us by using all sorts of imperfect people to do his work. It is a startling reminder that the church is a very human, frail, diverse institution, nonetheless charged with the mission to be the body of Christ, doing the work of Christ on earth.

That may be our best starting point: to acknowledge that we are an imperfect people who belong to an imperfect church, living in an imperfect world, trying to worship and serve a perfect God. What we keep forgetting, or keep refusing to remember, is our frail, sinful humanity, which is why God, in the fullness of time, became flesh and lived among us perfectly in Jesus, the Christ. The first disciples were far from perfect; they were temperamental, selfish, fickle, disloyal, unfaithful, and even quarrelsome with one another.

So how did we get here, to this point in time, as a church? That's where loyalty to the past demands our attention. No matter how much history has preceded us, most of us have a tendency to go back in time only as far as we can remember, and we tend to believe that time really began with our birth, so the past is primarily what we have experienced. Not so with the church—not so with Jesus. Time for Jesus began with God, and time for the church began when God made a promise—an agreement—a covenant with the Jews that God would be their God so long as the Jews would be faithful to God. The long history of God's dealing with the Jews set the stage for the coming of Jesus to establish, out of the tradition of Israel, the Christian tradition, and thus the church was born.

I hasten to admit all is not perfect in the church. It never has been and it never will be. But if ever there was a time for us in the church to be loyal to the past but open to the future, now is that time! Someone has said that God created time because we humans cannot learn everything at once. And someone also said God created memory so that we could have the past as our permanent teacher. And someone said God created the future because there is so much more that God wants to teach us and do through us.

The truth is that placing the blame may be a part of diagnosing any problem, but it is the prescription that actually produces the cure. So we need to keep going back to the source book: the Bible. The early church had its squabbles, its disagreements, its arguments, but always someone called them back to the past to get their point of departure for the future.

The church, almost at inception, was disrupted with theological and ecclesiastical controversies. Beyond the obvious power struggles between the Jewish and Gentile segments of the church, there was also the ever-present issue of who was the authentic spokesperson for the church.

Paul and Peter argued vehemently about whether or not these new Christians had to obey the laws of the Jews in order to be Christians. Paul argued with the elders in the early church because they let secular, unethical practices into the church. Paul argued against spiritual aberrations that detracted from faith in Jesus Christ.

As our text declares, from Paul: "Do not quench the Spirit. Do not despise the words of prophets, but test everything; hold fast to what is good; abstain from every form of evil." When Jesus was giving his final instructions to the disciples, when he was saying goodbye to them, he said, "When the Spirit of truth comes, he will guide you into all the truth . . . and he will declare to you the things that are to come" (John 16:13). In the side discussions at the General Assembly, one will hear phrases calling for a return to the old-fashioned gospel and to old-time religion. But that is a coward's way of thinking, because the Spirit of Jesus calls us not to live in the first century but to live by faith in Christ in the twenty-first century.

The Spirit of Jesus Christ is a living presence, and there is no evidence in existence that Jesus was ever guilty of favoritism. The love of Jesus that is God's love was for the whole human family. The cross stands forever showing forth the magnitude of that love. Jesus was always biased in favor of the power of that love to forgive, to heal, and to redeem. Jesus remains as the world's only authentic Savior. The resurrection of Jesus from death to life proves that when something goes wrong, it is a lot more important to find out who's going to fix it than who's to blame for it.

Alfred North Whitehead once declared: "The worst thing about quarrel is that it spoils a discussion." Far too frequently in the church, the Bible becomes not a truth to inform us but a tool to support our prejudices. Selective readings of the Bible can be far more dangerous than not reading the Bible at all. More wars, more prejudices, more hatred, more verbal violence, more

criticisms of others have been produced by selective Bible readings than by all the heresies combined. The Bible has been used
more often to bless and encourage vices than it has to change the
heart of individuals who are seeking a better way.

The Spirit of Christ is a living spirit, a Spirit who does not simply recite the faith of past centuries but who inspires and calls us
into the future. We sedate and somber Presbyterians would be
wise if we were to discover who this Spirit of Christ really is. The
Spirit of Christ is not some vague, dim figure who hides quietly
in the corridors of the past or behind the sacred walls. No, the
Spirit of Christ is a very powerful presence, motivating individuals and churches to be a powerful influence for God in a complex
and violent world.

A church that is alive, a living church, is made up of real people who, because they are real, do not always agree on every
issue. Two groups tend to be the dominant ones. There are those
who are traditionalist, conservative, resistant to change; and
there are those who, by temperament, are restless, impatient
with old ways, eager for change. Some of us find that there is a
bit of both groups in us. We want to be loyal to the past but we
want to be open to the future. And some of us believe the church
needs both groups if we are going to be loyal to the past but open
to the future. The future always grows out of the past. The one
thing we cannot do is to run off in all directions, because that will
destroy us. Nothing threatens us more than disunity!

One of Aesop's great fables illustrates this. Four oxen who
lived in a certain field were good friends. Sometimes a lion
would prowl around them. The oxen would put their tails
together so that when the lion came, he must face the horns of
one of them no matter from which direction he approached. But
after a while, the oxen began to disagree with one another and to
quarrel among themselves. Soon they separated and carelessly
went in different directions. The lion, finding them separated,
attacked one at a time and soon killed each one of them. Such
disunity threatens the church!

Jesus, in his final prayer with the disciples, prayed this way to
God: "I do not pray for these only"—meaning the Twelve—but

also for those who are to believe in me through their word, that they may all be one. And I do not pray, Father, that you should take them out of the world, but that you will keep them safe from the evil one" (John 17).

Never have we as Christians been more in need of the guidance of the Spirit of Christ—so that we can learn how to distinguish between what is new and good for the church and what is simply new but may destroy the church. If I had to explain in a single sentence the religious mood of today in this country, I think I would do it this way: there is a profound desire for God and for God's help with living, coupled with a deep distrust and rejection of all organized religion, which means the church! I frequently hear people say, "I've got my own religion, so I don't need the church." So also thought each of the oxen in Aesop's fable, which led to their individual destruction.

So our vision must begin with people and look to the church that believes in an unchanging Christ in an ever-changing world, that must once again grapple with its theology, its belief in Christ and Christ's hope for the human family. I believe the greatest challenge for the church today is to revive the biblical concept of community. John Winthrop's sermon "A Model of Christian Community" was delivered onboard ship in 1630, just before the people disembarked. In that sermon, Winthrop warned that if we pursue our pleasures and profits, we will surely perish out of this good land.

Paraphrasing the apostle Paul, Winthrop put it this way: "We are to entertain each other in brotherly affection, we must be willing to abridge ourselves of our superfluities, for the supply of others' necessities . . . we must delight in each other, make others' conditions our own, rejoice together, always having before our eyes our community as members of the same body."[1]

Obviously, we have ignored Winthrop's advice. Perhaps now more than ever before the church needs to discover what has caused the decline of the concept of community, an authentic faith community where the needs of one become the concern of all in that faith community.

The huge question is: What are people looking for from the

church? The crass answer is: Most don't know. Because of this, I must confess that the work of the church has a tendency to wear us out, to drain our energy, to exhaust our imagination, to stifle our ability to dream creatively and to plan wisely. We spend an exorbitant amount of energy and time trying to give to people what they think they want, when in the end it does not satisfy their most basic hunger. The hunger is spiritual in nature, and the unchanging Christ is what we must give to people.

This raises immediately the question: What should the church look like in the future? Hans Küng wrote this piece titled "The Church of the Future" and raises this question:

> To what kind of Christian, to what kind of church does the future belong? Not a church that is lazy, shallow, inefficient, timid and weak in its faith: not a church that expects blind obedience and fanatical party loyalty; not a church that is the slave of its own history, always putting on the brakes, suspiciously defensive and yet, in the end, forced into agreement; not a church that is blind to problems, suspicious of empirical knowledge yet claiming competent authority for everyone and everything; not a church that is quarrelsome, impatient and unfair in dialogue; not a church that is closed to the real world.
>
> In short, the future does not belong to a church that is dishonest!
>
> No, the future belongs: To a church that knows what it does not know; to a church that relies upon God's grace and wisdom and has in its weakness and ignorance a radical confidence in God; to a church that is strong in faith, joyous and certain yet self-critical; to a church filled with intellectual desire, spontaneity, animation and fruitfulness; to a church that has the courage of initiative and the courage to take risks; to a church that is completely open to the real world; to a church that is completely committed to Jesus Christ. In short, the future belongs to a thoroughly truthful church.[2]

So what is our goal, our purpose, our mission as a church? Our mission is to be a servant church, sharing the love of Christ with all people. It is brief; it is clear; it is precise; and it is why we exist as a church!

Loyal to the past, yes; but for Christ's sake, let us also be open to the future, because that is where Christ is—and if we believe that, one day, at the end of our life, we will be where Christ is, namely, with God, forever and forever, through all of eternity. Could you want more than that for all of God's people? And all of us are God's people, because God has made us and we all belong to God.

NOTES

1. In *Speeches That Changed the World*, compiled by Owen Collins (Louisville, Ky.: Westminster John Knox Press, 1999), 64.
2. Hans Küng, *The Church* (Garden City, N.Y.: Doubleday & Co., Image Books, 1976), 103–4.

To Bless the
Whole Human Family
Genesis 12:1–3; Luke 4:14–30

Robert A. Chesnut

Perhaps it will sound a bit strange to some of you, but do you know where I find some of my inspiration? From business authors! Most of you know how highly I think of Stephen Covey's *Seven Habits*.[1] I believe—no, I know—that the seven habits are profoundly faith-based and that they provide sound and practical guidance for personal and spiritual growth.

Another business author I find myself returning to again and again is Peter Senge of MIT, author of *The Fifth Discipline*.[2] That book focuses on what Senge calls "the learning organization." In the very beginning of his book he refers to the Greek word *metanoia*, used so frequently by Jesus in the Gospels. *Metanoia* is often translated as "repentance" or "conversion." It literally means a changed mind. It refers to a capacity for self-transcendence, self-correction, self-renewal. Senge says *metanoia* is the essential gift for those individuals and organizations that want to keep on learning and growing. Senge, by the way, also makes use in his work of spiritual capacities such as love, compassion, forgiveness, and reconciliation.

One of the most simple but effective illustrations of a speaker's point that I have ever witnessed was one used by Stephen Covey in a workshop he led in Pittsburgh a couple of years ago. There must have been three or four hundred of us present in a large meeting room at the David Lawrence Convention Center. Covey asked us all to do something that I'm going to ask all of you to do right now. First, please close your eyes and keep them closed. Now, raise your right hand high and point toward north. Keep on pointing. Now, open your eyes and look around. What do you see? All of us pointing in every conceivable direction at once! Right?

Now, I won't ask you to do next what Covey asked us to do next. You can just imagine it. "Stand up," he said, "and join hands. Now start moving together toward north!" Oh my gosh! How do we do that? Help! Does anyone have a compass? We need a compass!

Of course we need a compass. That was Covey's point, and the point of many business authors as well. The compass for the business organization, for any organization, and for individuals as well, says Covey, should be your mission statement. Your mission statement is your "big-picture" reason for being. It is your grand statement of purpose. It is your statement of where you're headed, your destination. Your mission statement is your compass, your North Star.

Now, it's interesting to me that the business world has taken over this concept of mission from us, from the church. And it's even more interesting, and even a bit ironic, that they often seem far more focused on their mission out there in the world of commerce than we are on ours here in the church. There is even greater irony here when you consider how much grander our mission is than theirs usually is. How on earth could you begin to get as fired up, as dedicated and enthused about your purpose as we Christians ought to be about ours, if you were in the business of manufacturing shoestrings or paperweights?

Maybe part of our problem is that we don't often enough stop to remind ourselves of what our mission is as the church of Jesus Christ. Just what is our *raison d'être*, our grand purpose, our guiding North Star? Our scripture readings this morning give us two major mission statements—an Old Testament mission statement and a New Testament mission statement. The Old

Testament statement is God's promise to Abraham and Sarah that he would bless them with a family, with many descendants, and that their family of faith would be a blessing to all the families of the earth.

Now, to bless, as the Old Testament understands blessing, is to bestow *shalom*. *Shalom* means not just peace as the absence of conflict. It means comprehensive well-being. It means inner harmony and harmony in our relationships. It means physical, emotional, spiritual health, wholeness. It means material security, freedom from want and fear. This is God's will for the whole human family, and it is our God-given mission as spiritual descendants of Abraham and Sarah to be God's agents in bringing divine blessing to all people worldwide. To paraphrase Saint Francis, "Lord, make us instruments of your blessing, agents of your *shalom* for the whole human family."

Now, to bless people must often entail delivering them from that which curses them, from that which makes their lives less than whole, from that which enslaves and exploits them, from that which brings dis-ease and death rather than full and abundant life. So deliverance is the focus of Jesus' mission statement that we heard this morning in Luke's Gospel.

The occasion here was the beginning of Jesus' public ministry. He had returned to his hometown synagogue in Nazareth, where he was invited to read the scripture. He chose the reading from the prophet Isaiah and then told the congregation that his God-given mission was bringing about the fulfillment of Isaiah's prophecy. God's Spirit had anointed Jesus as God's earthly agent of deliverance to bring good news to the poor, recovery of sight to the blind, release to the captives; to set at liberty the oppressed. Jesus was very much following in the tradition of the Old Testament mission statement, but his focus was on bringing the blessings of *shalom* to all those who had thus far been deprived of it, left out and left behind.

Now, then we find something very puzzling, and eventually very revealing, in this story in Luke. There appears to be a decidedly mixed reaction to Jesus' message. Initially, there seems to be some pride in a hometown boy made good; but the crowd quickly grows hostile, threatening even to push Jesus over a cliff.

What on earth is going on here? Well, it may be this: the problem may be that when Jesus read the famous passage from Isaiah, he left out a verse that expresses God's wrath against the Gentiles, the non-Jews. Furthermore, Jesus went on to cite some other Old Testament cases in which God showed special favor to Gentiles over Jews.

The sad fact is that the people of Nazareth were incensed to hear that God cares about the Gentiles, too. They were angered that Jesus should suggest that God cares about blessing and delivering anyone other than them, the chosen people. Jesus was pushing these people in his hometown to expand their vision, their mission, their notion of who it is that God cares about, who it is that God wants to bless and deliver. Jesus was pushing them hard to expand their inner circles. So they pushed back, pushed so hard that they very nearly killed Jesus right then and there, right at the start of his ministry, rather than three years later.

Jesus, you see, was calling for *metanoia,* for a change of heart and mind. He wanted to convert these folks back to the original vision, the original mission of Abraham's descendants—to bless all the people of the earth. But these "good" people of Nazareth wanted to think that they were God's chosen few, chosen for special privilege, not for a special mission to share God's blessing with all the families of the earth. They had become so hardhearted, so narrow-minded, so self-centered in their spiritual blindness that they were ready to kill before they would ever repent, convert.

This story of conflict about how we are to understand our mission goes on throughout the Bible. Those who truly got the message and understood the mission were often few and far between. But we do see glimpses of it in the Old Testament. We hear the prophet Isaiah envisioning a time when God's light will shine on the Gentiles, when all the families of the earth will be drawn together to God's house in Jerusalem. In the story of Jonah, we read of God's universal love for all people, even our enemies.

Jonah resisted God's mission to go and preach to the Assyrians so they would repent and be delivered from divine wrath. Jonah ran away because he hated the Assyrians and wanted them destroyed, not saved. But God caught up with Jonah and made him go do it anyway. And when his mission succeeded, when the Assyrians repented and were delivered from destruction, Jonah grieved about it. His own heart was still unconverted. He still wanted his enemies wiped out.

The struggle continues in the New Testament. There is the apostle Peter, for example, who simply could not believe that God wanted to include Gentiles in the Christian family unless they first became Jews and observed all the laws, both major and minor, of the Old Testament. Finally, it took a direct divine revelation to convert Peter, to change his heart and mind.

The struggle we are talking about this morning is the spiritual struggle between believing that God's blessing is just for us and for our kind and believing that we have a mission to share the blessing with everyone, especially with those who have been rejected, left out, and left behind—the least, the last, the lost.

I want to go back now to something that I mentioned at the outset. I said our mission statement is our statement of grand purpose, the "big picture" of what it is we're all about. The big picture is important because it's often so easy to get lost in the minor, distracting, even misleading details of it all.

We can say, for example, that the Bible is our road map, showing us where we ought to be headed, which way is north. But a big, detailed map by itself is not necessarily much help, is it? Not unless you have someone mark out the route for you—like an AAA Trip-Tik with the best interstates highlighted to get you to your destination. Otherwise, that big, complex map we call the Bible can be very confusing. It can even lead us off the track, into dead ends and onto neglected back roads that are no longer safe to travel.

I think that we can understand much of Jesus' teachings as an effort to highlight the big picture, to mark out a spiritual Trip-Tik for us. He rebuked the Pharisees for getting sidetracked, for straining out the gnats and swallowing the camels, for focusing on the jots and tittles of the law but overlooking the big picture therein, for knowing the letter but not the spirit of the law, for becoming self-righteous and judgmental toward others, for lacking humility and compassion, for drawing the circle of God's acceptance tightly around themselves alone.

Jesus looked at the book of Leviticus—a confusing tangle of ancient legal codes and taboos, mixing primitive superstitions together with enduring ethical insights—and what did he find there? He found laws in Leviticus forbidding a disabled person from being a priest, branding lepers as unclean outcasts from the human community, stigmatizing a woman as unclean during her menstrual period or after giving birth. Leviticus forbids same-sex relations, eating lobster, wearing clothes made of two different kinds of fabric, and planting a field with two different kinds of seed. Jesus looked at this tangle of moral interstates and back roads, and what did he lift out of Leviticus? This single verse: "You shall love your neighbor as yourself" (19:18b).

Then Jesus looked at Deuteronomy, another legal codebook, and he drew this single verse from it: "You shall love the Lord you God with all your heart, and with all your soul, and with all your might" (6:5). He put this verse together with his verse from Leviticus, and he gave us another big-picture mission statement: love God with all your being and your neighbor as yourself. Stay on that highway, Jesus says. Stay on that highway on your way to God's realm and you won't get lost.

The problem is that so many people, even today, major in the minors of the Bible. They turn it into a legalistic, moralistic codebook composed of all the jots and tittles. Then they use it as a big club to drive away from the gate of God's love all those unlike themselves whom they consider unworthy and unclean. So not only do they lose sight of God's grand purpose, not only do they become utterly lost and turned around in the back roads of the Bible, but they even become opponents of the good news, turning the message of blessing into one of curse for whole groups of God's beloved children.

In conclusion, I think we must continue to love these misguided souls as well. They, too, are God's beloved children. Jesus loved the Pharisees and wanted to deliver them too—from their spiritual enslavement to a loveless legalism.

Furthermore, we ourselves must avoid self-righteousness.

We, too, must be always mindful of our own need for *metanoia*, for converted hearts and minds. As Presbyterians, for example, we are especially prone to the sin of classism, social class pride and exclusivity. We liberal Presbyterians in particular often talk a very good game about God's special love for those left out and left behind, but our record of actually welcoming these very people into our congregations is deplorable. We talk the talk, but we don't walk the walk.

I remember an incident when I was a teenager active in our Westminster Youth Fellowship in my small Presbyterian congregation in western Oklahoma. The folks there were often of a mind-set similar to that in Jesus' hometown congregation. We were talking once about possible youth group activities. I suggested maybe we could get a pool table. The adult youth adviser immediately responded, "Oh no! That would attract the wrong kind of people!"

"Oh," I thought to myself, "isn't that what we Christians are supposed to be doing? Maybe Presbyterians have *different* instructions?"

Convert us again, O God. Turn us around and point us toward our North Star—your redeeming love for all people embodied in Christ. May that love be embodied in us, his church, his body. May we stand with open arms, welcoming one and all at the gate of your love. Filled and anointed by your Spirit, may we follow Christ's way of compassion and deliverance, healing and reconciliation. Lord, make us instruments of your blessing, agents of your *shalom* for the *whole* human family.

NOTES

1. Stephen R. Covey, *The Seven Habits of Highly Effective People* (New York: Simon & Schuster, 1989); also *The Seven Habits of Highly Effective Families* (New York: Golden Books, 1997).
2. Peter Senge, *The Fifth Discipline: The Art and Practice of the Learning Organization* (New York: Doubleday & Co., 1990).

PART 3

God's
People Sent

Becoming the
Salt and the Light

John M. Buchanan

Anyone who spends any time around the church—not "church" in the abstract but the institutional church, with its worn-out linoleum floors and its nineteenth-century hymns, its propensity to trivialize the gospel and its tendency to make mountains out of molehills, and what is far worse, molehills out of mountains, and its use of its own message of love and redemption to be unlovely and exclusive and sometimes downright hateful—anyone who knows anything about the institutional church becomes quickly impatient with it and sometimes sick at heart over it. Those who continue to love the church want it to be so much more than it is—more biblical, more faithful, more inclusive, more relevant, more Christocentric, friendlier, bigger, more evangelical.

Author and Presbyterian minister Frederick Buechner wrote, "Maybe the best thing that could happen to the church would be for some great tidal wave of history to wash it all away, the church buildings tumbling, the church money all lost, blowing through the air like dead leaves, the differences between preachers and congregations all lost too. Then all we would have left would be each other and Christ, which was all there was in the first place."[1]

But even Buechner's draconian scenario isn't radical enough, because the simple fact is that the earliest church never quite lived up to Jesus' hopes for it or our routine romanticization of it. And, one assumes, it never lived up to its own expectations of itself, either.

With a twinkle in her eye, author Annie Dillard, who spent time as an adolescent sitting in the balcony of a Presbyterian church in Pittsburgh and therefore speaks from authentic experience, says:

> What a pity, that so hard on the heels of Christ came the Christians. There is no breather. The disciples turn into the early Christians between one rushed verse and another. What a dismaying pity, that here come the Christians already, flawed to the core, full of wild ideas and self-importance. . . . They set out immediately to take over the world and they pretty much did it. They converted emperors, raised armies, lined their pockets with real money, and did evil things large and small, in century after century, including this one. They are smug and busy, just like us and who could believe in them?[2]

A New Way of Life

It turns out that Frederick Buechner and Annie Dillard and many people like them, including me, assume most of the people who will read this book have not given up on the church. And the reason is that every now and then the church speaks the truth; and the truth, as Jesus promised, sets men and women free. Every now and then the church puts its money where its mouth is and invests in the welfare of its community—loves the world in the same way its Lord did, and the world somehow becomes a little more of what God created it to be. Every now and then, in fact, with quiet consistency, day in and day out, year after year, century after century, the church proclaims the good news of God's love in Jesus Christ and then actually expresses that love, incarnates that love, and human life is saved, recovered, reformed, celebrated, challenged, reimagined, reanimated, renewed, re-created.

It is fashionable to critique the church for the negative impact its presence and mission have had on the life of the world. It is politically correct to acknowledge that the Christian church has been elitist and imperialistic and has superimposed Western values, Western culture, on people of other cultures in its missionary enterprise.

But there is another way to tell that story without denying the accuracy and appropriateness of the critique. From the very beginning, the Christian church was conspicuous by the way it bridged the gaps that divided the cultures of the first century: gaps of gender, age, race, social status, religion, morality. The early church was conspicuous, as was its Lord, because of its inclusivity. The early Christians, in addition to their flaws and foibles, ate together, learned together, prayed together, and actually began to care about and for one another in a way the world recognized. "See how they love one another," people said when they looked at the church.

The first and best evangelism project of the church turns out to be the quality of life lived in the world: "They devoted themselves to the apostles' teaching and fellowship, to the breaking of bread and the prayers. . . . [T]hey broke bread at home and ate their food with glad and generous hearts, praising God and having the goodwill of all the people" (Acts 2:42, 46b-47a).

Kenneth Woodward, religion writer for *Newsweek*, wrote an essay on the millennium, "2000 Years of Jesus," that highlights critical changes in history that happened because of Christianity and the Christian church. "Like a supernova, the initial impact of Christianity on the ancient Greco-Roman world produced shock waves that continued to register long after the Roman Empire disappeared."[3]

The Christian church introduced a new idea of God to the world. Out of its own Hebrew theological heritage, it proclaimed the good news of a God who relates to individual women and men and children in a personal and intimate way, a God who loves like a nursing mother and a waiting father. The church, because of its basic theology, began to practice, demonstrate, and proclaim the worth and value of individual human life.

The early Christian church protected the children. Under

Roman law, fathers could choose to keep or to abandon a new-born. Female babies were particularly vulnerable. A study of grave sites at Delphi revealed that of six hundred upper-class families, only a half dozen raised more than one daughter. Unwanted children were simply "cast out," abandoned in the streets to die of exposure. The early Christian church became an orphanage for the unwanted babies.[4]

I often wonder what his friends thought when Jesus called them salt and light: "You are the salt of the earth; but if salt has lost its taste, how can its saltiness be restored? It is no longer good for anything, but it is thrown out and trampled under foot. You are the light of the world. A city built on a hill cannot be hid. No one after lighting a lamp puts it under the bushel basket, but on the lampstand, and it gives light to all in the house" (Matt. 5:13–15).

New Testament scholars continue to study those provocative metaphors, and every preacher knows not only the standard interpretations but also their rich potential for sermonizing. They are deceptively modest, functional metaphors. Salt and light—both, in spite of their modesty, have profound effects on their environment. Salt preserves. It changes food, makes it tastier, livelier, zestier. A salt-free diet can be bland and uninteresting. Light abolishes darkness. The darker the darkness, the more visible the light, even a tiny candle. You need light in order to see. You need light to find your way home, or wherever it is you are going.

"You are the salt of the earth. . . . You are the light of the world," Jesus told his disciples, and I've always wondered what they thought about it, what we think about it today. The great temptation of Christianity and the Christian church has always been to get out of the world, figuratively or literally. Followers of Jesus have always been tempted to give up on the world, reject the world, retreat from the world—to a monastery, a mountain-top, the comfort of their own insular community protected by gothic stone walls, esoteric vocabulary, or inaccessible buildings, liturgies, rites, and regulations.

"You are salt and light," Jesus told his first friends. He commissioned them with those metaphors to resist the temptation to withdraw and called them to become his followers, his disciples, his women and men in the world, to be seasoning and light to those around them.

It was a lesson to which he returned. At a critical juncture in the gospel story, Jesus took his closest friends, Peter, James, and John, up onto a mountaintop. Peter, just six days earlier, had responded to Jesus' question "Who do you say that I am?" with the breathtaking affirmation "You are the Messiah, the Son of the living God." But very shortly thereafter Peter showed that he did not understand at all the meaning and implication of his startling declaration, when he refused to accept Jesus' explanation that he must suffer and die. The incident ended powerfully with Jesus' sharpest rebuke of his close friend: "Get behind me, Satan! You are a stumbling block to me" (Matt. 16:23).

And so it was an important gesture when Peter, along with James and John, was invited to go with Jesus to the mountain. While they were there, one of the most mysterious incidents in the gospel narrative occurred: "And he was transfigured before them, and his face shone like the sun, and his clothes became dazzling white" (Matt. 17:2). Jesus' identity was affirmed and Peter's bold declaration was confirmed by the appearance of heroic and messianic figures from the past, Moses and Elijah. Once again, Peter misunderstood, this time wanting to preserve the mysterious moment of revelation on the mountain by building booths. And again, Jesus rebuked Peter, more gently this time, by ignoring his suggestion and leading Peter and the others down from the mountain of transfiguration to the valley, where there was a crowd of people waiting for them, among them a desperate father with an epileptic son. The word here is strong and pointed. The disciples want to stay on the mountain, isolated, away from the distractions of life, free to reflect and pray and meditate and receive God's gift of revelation. The disciples want to withdraw from the ambiguities of the world. But Jesus won't allow it. Instead, Jesus leads them back down to a waiting crowd and urgent human need.

Near the end of the story, the motif emerges again. Jesus

decided to go to Jerusalem, "set his face to go to Jerusalem" (Luke 9:51). The disciples were reluctant, afraid, preferring the safety of life in Galilee. The disciples want to stay in security. Jesus goes on ahead of them to the city, the capital, the fulcrum of the nation's life, Jerusalem.

Dietrich Bonhoeffer, in his Nazi prison cell, wrote to his parents on the day after the assassination attempt on Adolf Hitler failed, and therefore on the day he knew, with certainty, that he was going to die: "During the last year or so I have come to appreciate the worldliness of Christianity as never before. I thought I could acquire faith by trying to live a holy life, or something like it. Later I discovered and am still discovering up to this very moment, that it is only by living completely in the world, that one learns to believe."[5]

The Church in the World

Learning to be a faithful follower of Jesus means living more deeply in the world. It is an important moment in the journey of discipleship. Jesus Christ does not want us, or his church, to withdraw from life in order to be faithful to him. In fact, Jesus wants us to plunge more deeply and intentionally into life. The faithful Christian life is not one of adhering to a list of prohibitions; faith does not diminish one's life. To the contrary, Jesus Christ is God's great "Yes!" to life. The incarnation is God's great affirmation of human life. The gospel narrative is the story of God loving the world and saving the world. Following Jesus, trusting Jesus, as individuals and as church, means living more intentionally, more passionately; exposing oneself to more life, more pain, more suffering, more joy, more agony, more ecstasy, more tears, more laughter—and most important, more love.

"You are the salt of the earth . . . the light of the world," he told them. It is why the church exists in the first place: to be salt and light in and for the world; to live not for itself but for the world. "The church exists for mission as fire exists for burning," Emil Brunner put it.

The story of the church following Jesus into the world in mission is inspiring. In the Republic of Korea there is a strong and life-giving Christian church because of the faithful work of missionaries who knew their calling to love and serve the world in addition to proclaiming good news and recruiting church members. When Horace Underwood arrived from America in the late 1880s, he founded churches and Severance Hospital in Korea. And when, several years later, Korea was stricken by a virulent cholera epidemic, physicians and nurses from the new Christian hospital began to care for the sick and dying. The impact was impressive. The standard method for dealing with infectious disease before that time was to isolate infectious persons, often totally abandoning the sick and dying to face pain and death alone. Korean people were astonished to see Christians ministering to cholera victims, risking infection and death because of something they believed about God and God's love in Jesus Christ. When Western Christians ask Korean church leaders about the phenomenal growth of the church in Korea, the response always includes the clear identification of the missionaries with the Korean people. The Christian church, from the outset, left its buildings and institutions to stand with the Korean people in times of need, crisis, conflict, and suffering, beginning with the cholera epidemic and continuing during the Japanese invasion, occupation, and persecution. The Korean church has distinguished itself and successfully proclaimed the good news, sustaining steady and strong growth because of its focus on the mission of Jesus Christ in the world. Today the Korean church operates universities and hospitals and has an ambitious global mission enterprise of its own.

"You are the salt of the earth . . . the light of the world," Jesus told his disciples. The church in the Balkans lives out those metaphors with heroic faithfulness in the midst of war, ethnic cleansing, and a deep racism that casts a shadow on the future. In Ocijek, Croatia, the Croatian Reformed Church, in collaboration with ecumenical partners including the Presbyterian Church (U.S.A.), provides a theological seminary for Reformed students from many countries whose governments regard one another with suspicion and hostility. The Agape Project provides food and shelter for the thousands of refugees who characterize the entire region: Bosnian Muslims, Serbian Orthodox Christians, Croatian Catholics. Bosnian Muslim refugees are mostly women, children, and elderly men. Young men and boys have disappeared. At an Agape feeding center in Ocijek, Muslim women bring whatever containers they can find—bottles, kettles, scrub buckets—and stand in line to receive soup and a loaf of bread. An old woman, a Muslim, asked who was providing the food was told that it was American Christians. With tears in her eyes, she said, "Tell them my husband and son were shot, my home was destroyed. I have nothing. Tell them that without this food I would starve to death. Tell them I say, 'God bless them.' "

The Agape Project is a heroic example of Christians following their Lord into the world to its most desperate and neediest places. One of Agape's projects is rebuilding destroyed villages and resettling the people who were driven out of them by armed forces. Plans for the reconstruction of a Muslim village included assembling materials, money, and labor to rebuild every structure that had been destroyed in the sustained bombardment. The Muslim village chief, or mayor, who was consulting with a representative of Agape, noted that Agape was planning to rebuild the Islamic mosque, which had been blown to bits. "Why would you Christians who have been trying to convert us for a thousand years want to rebuild our mosque?" he asked. The Agape representative was able to explain that Christians will rebuild an Islamic mosque because we follow a Lord who orders us to love neighbors as ourselves; a Lord who told about a good man, a member of a despised racial minority, who knelt by the roadside to save the life of one who had been brutally beaten; a Lord who did not inquire about an individual's religious identity before healing, helping, and restoring. "You are the salt of the earth . . . the light of the world," Jesus said. The church is called to be in mission, sent into all the world in the name of Jesus Christ.

Local congregations as well as denominational mission agencies are called to be in the world. Distinguished University of Chicago sociologist Jean Bethke Elshtain argues that the very existence of a church building, even one that is closed twenty-four hours per day, has a positive and measurable effect on the health of the surrounding neighborhood. And churches with open doors and programs to meet the needs of neighbors are usually vital, healthy, and, many times, growing churches. It was not only for the sake of the world that Jesus called his disciples salt and light. It was for their own spiritual growth and faith and health.

A recent study conducted by the Church Growth Strategy Team of the Presbyterian Church (U.S.A.) revealed that growing churches share one common characteristic—a commitment to mission in the world. In spite of theological and liturgical diversity, growing mainline churches are extending their love and compassion and concern for justice into the neighborhoods and cities, the nation and the world. Mission is the key. Housing for the homeless, community feeding programs, day care for children or the elderly, Head Start, after-school tutoring programs for children—vital churches are in mission. Mission seems to be the healthy, life-giving ingredient. And the opposite is sadly obvious. Declining churches, for one reason or another, are not ordinarily extending themselves into the world but rather are absorbing all their spiritual, emotional, physical, and monetary resources in the struggle to survive.

Jesus called his disciples the salt of the earth and the light of the world. It is the mission of the people and the institution that claim his name to be in the world as radically and courageously as he was. It is the mission of his church to be salt and light.

Finding the Way Home

Light is necessary to see, to know where one is, to find one's way. A light in the window is a sign of welcome, of hospitality, of home.

The world desperately needs an institution with a heart and soul big enough to give itself to its mission and, at the same time, to be the light of welcome and homecoming. The world desperately needs someone to be what Jesus called his followers to be—a place of consistent grace and unconditional love. We live in a violent world: a world in which hate groups use the new communications potential of the Internet to spread their ideas of racial purity and racial violence; a world in which the phrase "ethnic cleansing" describes an appalling new reality—governments and paramilitary organizations working to exterminate entire populations because of ethnic, tribal, and religious identity.

Politically and socially, we seem to be caught in a new paradigm of win-lose. Every issue, every difference of opinion, every modest conflict is inflated to major proportions, with winning at all costs being the new moral imperative. Those who disagree with prevailing opinions or conventional wisdom are enemies who must be destroyed. It has become a hard world in which older virtues of civility and propriety and respect for one's opponent are increasingly rare. A professor at Georgetown University, Deborah Tannen, says that Americans have developed a "corrosive, contentious, argument culture—attacking and destroying opponents has become the mantra of the day."[6]

Even religious institutions reflect this new phenomenon. Denominational meetings, General Assemblies, annual conferences, which used to be best characterized as wonderful family reunions, increasingly feel like contentious confrontations, political and ideological battlefields where every issue is debated, evaluated, and then voted on the basis of ideological impact.

The world desperately needs what Jesus called his followers to be: salt and light—the light of hospitality, a community of people who love one another and show the world how to love.

Theologian William Placher argues that the purpose of religious denominations is to be communities of love and acceptance, unity in diversity where individuals feel welcome and affirmed, not battlefields where we fight one another over the "hot-button" issues of the day until one side wins and the other slinks away in defeat or withdraws altogether. Denominations, Placher said, are places where theology means more than ideology—"places in our society where people from widely diverse places across the political spectrum can talk about substantial issues within the context of an ongoing community of shared beliefs." Referring to the most difficult and contentious issues that threaten to divide the churches, Placher says, "If we can keep these conversations going, we mainline Protestants will make a major contribution to holding this fragmenting society of ours together."[7]

How are we going to do this? How are we going to be the salt of the earth and, at the same time, a community of acceptance and respect that provides the light of true community in a desperately needy world?

We might begin by thinking in a new way about these precious institutions of ours called churches. We might actually stop evaluating them in the way our market culture models for us, that is, on the basis of productivity and profitability, membership rolls and budgets, and actually start looking at how much love and compassion and justice are being done in the world. And we might actually start to think anew about the church as the only way we have of living out the good news of God's love in Jesus Christ, in community, not as one more arena in which to do ideological battle with opponents.

Author Anne Lamott describes her return to faith and the church in her book *Traveling Mercies*. It is the story of a small church being salt of the earth and light of the world in a remarkably life-transforming and life-saving way. The book is dedicated to the people of that small congregation, who took her in and affirmed her and loved her in a time of desperate personal need.

Lamott tells a story about church as salt of the earth and light of the world. A seven-year-old girl became lost one day. She "ran up and down the streets of the big town where they lived, but she couldn't find a single landmark. She was very frightened. Finally, a policeman stopped to help her. He put her in the passenger seat of his car and they drove around until she finally saw her church. She pointed it out to the policeman, and then she told him firmly, 'You could leave me out now. This is my church, and I can always find my way home from here.' "[8]

How are we to become salt of the earth and light of the world? Nowhere does the biblical tradition suggest that doing God's will is merely a matter of trying harder. Rather, the gracious invitation of the Gospel is to allow God's love in Jesus Christ to work in transforming ways in the lives of individuals and in the life of the church. And so, perhaps what we most need to do is invite Jesus to be part of our churches, listen to him, do what he tells us to do, and be what he calls us to be.

> We are Your people:
> Lord, by your grace,
> You dare to make us
> Christ to our neighbors
> of every nation and race.
>
> Lord, as we minister
> in different ways,
> may all we're doing
> show that You're living,
> meeting Your love with our praise.[9]

NOTES

1. Frederick Buechner, *The Clown in the Belfry* (San Francisco: Harper San Francisco, 1992), 158.
2. Annie Dillard, "The Gospel according to Saint Luke," in *Incarnation: Contemporary Writers on the New Testament*, ed. Alfred Corn (New York: Viking, 1990), 36.
3. Kenneth L. Woodward, "2000 Years of Jesus," *Newsweek*, March 29, 1999.
4. John D. Crossan, *Jesus: A Revolutionary Biography* (San Francisco: Harper, 1994), 62–64.
5. Dietrich Bonhoeffer, in letter of July 21, 1944, *Letters and Papers from Prison* (New York: Macmillan Co., 1953).
6. *Chicago Tribune* Book Review, March 29, 1998. Quoted in review of Deborah Tannen, *The Argument Culture: Moving from Debate and Dialogue* (New York: Random House, 1998).
7. William Placher, "Sticking Together," *Christian Century* (April 22–29, 1998), 421.
8. Anne Lamott, *Traveling Mercies: Some Thoughts on Faith* (New York: Pantheon Books, 1999), 55.
9. Brian Wren, "We Are Your People," *The Presbyterian Hymnal* (Louisville, Ky.: Westminster John Knox Press, 1990), no. 436. Copyright © 1975 by Hope Publishing Co.

The Great Commission

Progress Report

William H. Hopper, Jr.

Church Growth

The Christian church today is 1.9 billion strong, on the verge of 2 billion at the millennium![1] No one knows how many millions of Christians there are in China, but we do know that the 3-Self Movement in China estimates that an average of six and a half churches have been opened or reopened somewhere in China every day since 1979.[2] No one knows how many Christians there are in Africa, but we do know that Christians in the Southern Hemisphere are rapidly overtaking the number of Christians in Europe and North America combined.

And so it goes. There are more Presbyterians in Korea than there are in the Presbyterian Church (U.S.A.). Two congregations in Seoul have fifty thousand members each. Despite war, famine, persecution, and refugee flight across the southern part of their country, the number of Christians in the Sudan has multiplied ten times in the decade of the 1990s. The fact that the Presbyterian Church (U.S.A.) has been losing members in recent years does *not* mean that the world Christian community has lost vitality!

When I was growing up in the Presbyterian Church, the marching orders of the church were found in the Great

Commission: "Go therefore and make disciples of all nations" (Matt. 28:19–20). The Presbyterian Church (U.S.A.) has taken seriously its mission challenge and responsibility, so that it is not too much to say that, in the providence of God and under the guidance and blessing of the Holy Spirit, the Great Commission is being fulfilled. Oh yes, there have been tragic mistakes, serious lacks in sensitivity to people in some places, and spectacular failures from time to time, but with all that, there is every reason to rejoice that the good news of Jesus Christ has been proclaimed so that there is a church in every country on the planet!

Church Witness in Social Justice Issues

In the last decade of its first century, concluded in 1965, the Presbyterian Church in Taiwan doubled its membership. It has since doubled that number again. But that is far from the whole story. This denomination has long pushed for human rights and justice for all peoples, particularly for native Taiwanese; peace with justice; and stewardship of the land. The church has stressed social service through the typical means of education and medicine, but it has fought prostitution tourism and such things as political exclusion with a demand for democratic process and institutions. The general secretary of the church at the time, Dr. C. M. Kao, was a political prisoner for many months when the government tried to break the church's human rights efforts. The associate stated clerk of our General Assembly visited Dr. Kao in prison, symbolizing our solidarity with those who seek to follow Jesus' call to mission (Luke 4).

Typically, immediately after the devastating September 1999 earthquake in Taiwan, several things happened in the Presbyterian Church. Each congregation became engaged in direct earthquake relief and sent money and/or people to the worst-hit areas to serve, and special prayer services were held throughout the denomination. The Tainan and Taipei seminaries took time off so students, faculty, and administration could help personally. The General Assembly offices put aside all other business to provide immediate assistance. Financial aid was offered in many places.[3]

The Presbyterian Church (U.S.A.) must never forget its policy of "Mission Responsibility Through Investment" and its significant involvement to assist in the struggle against apartheid in South Africa, among other social-justice efforts here and abroad. Our denomination's role in *not* investing funds held by the General Assembly, including those funds held by the Board of Pensions and the Presbyterian Foundation, in companies that were doing business in South Africa helped in the victory for majority rule of Africans. Pressure also was put on the Reformed Church in South Africa to integrate worship and all its activities. Racial justice was the key.

Few Presbyterians seem to be aware of the centuries-old effort by the Waldensian Church in Italy for religious, social, and political rights for all citizens in Italy, as well as the sustained effort in earlier centuries for freedom to practice evangelism and worship throughout much of central and southern Europe. Rarely throughout all of history have Christians been more gallant and courageous against great odds in seeking social justice, education, and human rights for all persons than have the Waldensians, who trace their history to Lyon, France, where in 1176, Peter Valdez had the audacity to preach to the poor—and without a license from the established church! The PC(USA) is proud to encourage Waldensians in partnership in mission, as they support us. (A partner church is one with which our denomination has official relations, most of which have or have had PC(USA) missionaries working with them.)

The United Church of Christ in Thailand, composed of many members who have roots in Presbyterian Church (U.S.A.) mission work, is engaged in an outstanding ministry in Chiang Mai among those with AIDS and their families, in seeking to prevent the spread of AIDS, and in treating those who are HIV positive. In earlier years in that same city, the emphasis was on a ministry with those who suffered from leprosy and with their families.

Mission Is Not All One Way

For many years, the Synod of the Covenant (Ohio and Michigan) annually has had a number of guests—call them missionaries—from partner churches around the world to work with presbyteries, congregations, youth conferences, and the like for a period of months. This synod and these overseas churches understand that our denomination is not only a sending church but a receiving church, as we both teach and learn. As has been the case throughout history, we openly receive Christians from other nations. Each year some seventy-five persons come from partner churches to work in our denomination, in seminaries and colleges and in the Synod of the Covenant.

In a recent situation, our denomination made it financially possible for the church in Venezuela to "lend" one of its outstanding leaders to be principal (president) of the seminary in Colombia, in what we call three-way mission. We do not try to do it all, but we seek to enable mission.

The Independent Presbyterian Church of Brazil has extended its agreement with San Gabriel Presbytery in California to continue to pay a large portion of the cost of a new church development in the Portuguese language, a ministry under the leadership of a minister of the Brazilian church. The Presbytery of Tainan in Taiwan also helps financially a Taiwanese-language church development in the same California presbytery. It seems as if every presbytery in our land has at least one ethnic minority congregation within its boundaries with worship conducted in a language other than English. It is our stated denominational effort to seek to increase dramatically the number of ethnic minority congregations; specific goals are adopted regularly.

PC(USA) Mission Personnel

One of the best kept secrets in the Presbyterian Church (U.S.A.) is the large number of persons who are eager and willing to serve with our denomination overseas or in the United States. In one year, when I was the staff person responsible for our denominational office of mission personnel, we kept a record of the number of applicants, and we were astounded—the number was 5,621! These were young, old, and middle-aged, and of course, relatively few of that number finally were appointed. Some were discouraged by the prolonged application and orientation process. Many did not have the necessary qualifications or experience requested by the partner churches who ask for our personnel. Some did not pass the physical or psychological examination process. The sad part is that partner churches were requesting far more persons than the budget of the Worldwide Ministries Division could afford. Most years, the problem is one of finance. The requests are there; the personnel are available; but the funds are not. We have consistently sought to recruit the best persons to represent us around the world in mission.

In a consultation one year with the two Presbyterian churches of the Democratic Republic of Congo (then called Zaire), the general secretary of the larger denomination presented a request list for about half the number of persons we had appointed the previous year for the whole world. I was designated to respond by stating that we could appoint that year for all churches only about three times the number that he wanted for his country, so a priority list had to be prepared. He replied, "These are all priorities." Then he said, "Whether the missionaries come with money"—he knew that money often follows missionaries—"or they have no modern technical skills, we still want them because they represent for us our relation with the rest of the Christian community."

I admit to prejudice. I urge young (or older) Presbyterians who wish to serve overseas or in the United States to apply for service with the PC(USA) and not through other groups. For one thing, there is accountability. Every PC(USA) missionary is accountable to a governing body of our church, as the Worldwide Ministries Division represents the General Assembly, and all ordained persons are accountable to their presbyteries as well. No missionary operates outside the governing-body system.

There also is financial accountability. The General Assembly *Minutes* annually display how every dollar is spent. Anyone who disagrees with the financial decisions can object through the prescribed process at the annual General Assembly, which is composed of commissioners from each presbytery. The figures are spread out for all to see. All gifts go directly for the causes to which they are given, and a tracer is put on any problem that arises. There is no doubt where the money goes.

On policy issues, Presbyterian-related missionaries work within guidelines that have been tried and honed. Though not always perfect, policies are based on theological principles and experience worldwide, today in some eighty countries. Unlike many others, Presbyterians work with the national church of the country where they are sent, believing that in God's economy it is the national church of each nation that has the vision and responsibility for that place. It is sometimes arrogant and chauvinistic for us in the United States to think that we know so much better than Christians in their own land what is needed. Of course, we disagree at times with other denominations, and we struggle with them. Sometimes our position prevails; at other times our convictions lose. But we maintain a relationship that seeks to honor our sisters and brothers in Christ. Instead of seeking converts by the numbers, we seek to be God's agents in trying to bring into being a national church in every land.

Not only is the missionary the agent of the church; the church is there to support and care for the missionary in times of need. I may be one of the few missionaries who has had to come home for health reasons from two countries. The Presbyterian Church (U.S.A.) was there for me and my family, for which I am eternally grateful. We have a mutually supportive relationship— denomination and missionary.

Further, our denomination is responsible for those who must learn the language, the culture, the habits, and the customs of the people and for such things as the care and education of missionary children. No one should go overseas without having studied the history of the country and without knowing something about and having respect for the people of the predominant religions. Orientation is never enough, but it is vital.

In all candor, a word needs to be said about the sexual orientation of missionaries, as that subject seems to consume so much church thought in our era. There probably has never been a time

in history when there were not gay and lesbian missionaries—
Presbyterian and otherwise. The vocation often has been for single persons as well as couples. Doubtless many, if not most, gay
and lesbian persons were not practicing homosexuals overseas.
There certainly have been such persons during the years I served
overseas, beginning in 1947, and there certainly were during my
time in the personnel office.

Perhaps the surprising thing for some is that I know of but one
instance when national Christians seemed to have questions
about a possibly gay missionary, and the questions were largely
unrelated to that person's sexual orientation. I never learned
whether that man was gay or not. Legally, we could not ask. Our
missionaries never had to declare themselves one way or
another, and they were accepted for their Christian faith and
calling as demonstrated by their faithfulness in their vocation
and in their lives. One would presume that sensitive national
Christians were aware of the sexual orientation of most missionaries, but the missionaries were accepted regardless.

Certainly, the reverse is true. When a representative of a partner church comes to this country to work, no one inquires about
his or her sexual orientation. The same surely is true when students from partner churches come for additional training or
education under the magnificent leadership development program of the Worldwide Ministries Division of our church; no one
asks such questions, and the student returns, in time, to her or
his own nation and church.

A Few Current Challenges

1. It is surprising how few USA Presbyterians seek to make
contact with the national church of the country they are visiting
or working in overseas or with Presbyterian professional workers
in that country. Materials and information are available for each
country and its denominations through the Worldwide
Ministries Division in Louisville. Further, relatively few tourists
take advantage of the outstanding Presbyterian mission study
tours overseas, which usually are more insightful—and
cheaper—than commercial tours. Traveling in other countries

and living overseas, Presbyterian church members can be effective and genuine missionaries in their own attitudes and witness.

2. For prayer purposes, if for nothing else, the annual *Mission Yearbook for Prayer and Study* is informative about our Christian sisters and brothers in other lands, their work, challenges, and mission. This generation of USA Presbyterians seems better informed about political affairs in countries where we have partner churches than about the churches in those countries. No Sunday worship service should fail to include prayer for persons in other lands, as well as those in one's own neighborhood, for we all are world citizens.

3. Foreign students and immigrants from other lands welcome genuine hospitality when they come to our land, and we have untold opportunities to provide assistance, including inviting them into our homes and churches. Shopping, visiting doctors, locating government offices, and applying for a driver's license all seem routine to those of us familiar with our procedures and places of doing business, but such things can seem strange to newcomers and provide opportunities for genuine hospitality. Teaching English as a second language can also be immensely helpful.

4. Racial and religious prejudice have not yet fled our shores. We are not required to laugh at jokes at the expense of Poles or Arabs, the handicapped or Native Americans, much less to tell such stories. Murders of homosexuals, Jews, African Americans, and others happen with horrifying frequency in our culture, so each Christian has full responsibility to monitor his or her own behavior and to encourage others to be charitable to all persons who are in any way different from us. With our tongues we can torture minorities and foreigners in the same way that terrorists maim and kill.

Where Are We, Then, in Mission Early in This Century?

Countless congregations are now engaged in local mission in all kinds of ways, many unknown before the mid–twentieth century. This development in the past half century is remarkable and is to be highly commended. Mission now is much more realistically understood to begin with each member, and not with some special class of people sent somewhere else.

Two tragic losses, however, have accompanied this trend:

1. Churches have largely disappeared from the heart of the nation's cities so that congregations are much less visible downtown, and the sense of ministry "where cross the crowded ways of life" comes from suburban areas outside the encounter, rather than from congregations within the inner city.

2. Our tendency as a nation and as a church has been to become isolationist, as we have de-emphasized the charge to "go into all the world." Presbyterian adults commonly are heard to say something like "I think we must minister to our own first." We often fail to realize that "our own" are God's people all over the planet.

The trumpet sounds an uncertain note about the nature of our proclamation. We are much more likely to debate the nature of our call and our mission than we are to proclaim boldly, "Jesus Christ is Lord." Happily, the heart of the Christian message is less triumphalist than its simplistic statements in past days would indicate. We are aware that God has chosen to speak to people through other great religions, but we are not nearly so certain what to say to non-Christians and how to say it in relevant and clear ways. Somehow, while recognizing that God may have revealed God's self in a variety of other ways, we have not yet learned how to articulate boldly that "for me and my house, we will serve the Lord," because the way in which God has been revealed to us is through the redeeming love and grace of Jesus Christ.

Our nationalistic tendencies and our uncertainties about our message have the powerful result of blurring our concern about such things as a military coup in Pakistan in 1999. Perhaps for most of us, when we learn of such developments, our immediate concerns are likely to be about recent American foreign policy issues and the potential effects on our trade, taxes, and investments, rather than about the possible consequences for the Presbyterian Church of Pakistan.

104 John M. Buchanan

But what do we know about the Christian community in that country today, much less about the particularities of the blasphemy law that jeopardizes the life of every Christian and Christian village when any word remotely criticizing Muhammad or Islam is uttered? As a Christian denomination with few Presby-terian missionaries in a given nation, we have become isolated from the realities of the Christian church in many countries.

We rejoice when we hear of particular missionary examples of outstanding work, as well we should; but we dare not forget that national Christians in nation after nation are the ones who bear the brunt of discrimination and sometimes oppression and persecution. While recognizing that our church—often in cooperation with other denominations like ours—historically has been the human means for planting and developing national churches worldwide, it is the Christians in those lands who are the primary agents now for their church growth and development.

Many Presbyterians are giving thanks for the international leadership-development program of our Worldwide Ministries Division, a program that seeks to respond to requests from partner churches by assisting them in training their own members for specific positions of leadership within their churches.[4] Part of that story is told in a wonderful new book *And God Gave the Increase*, edited by June Ramage Rogers. Indeed, we all should recognize anew that the mission of the church is a joyous mission. We are not primarily and obviously a happy church, but we dare not allow our infighting and political rhetoric to overwhelm us. We must adopt anew our living conviction that "our chief end is to glorify God forever." We must sing again!

NOTES

1. David B. Barrett and Todd M. Johnson, *International Bulletin of Missionary Research,* January 1999, 25.
2. *China News Update,* Pasadena, California, May 1999, 6; and from an address by the general secretary of the China Christian 3-Self Movement, in Los Angeles, California, June 1999.

3. Statement from Presbyterian Disaster Assistance Office, Louisville, Kentucky, September 23, 1999.
4. June Ramage Rogers, ed., *And God Gave the Increase* (Louisville, Ky.: Worldwide Ministries Division, Presbyterian Church (U.S.A.), undated). Presbyterian Distribution Service (PDS) #74320-98-001.

Mud and Meeting People

John 9:1–21

Anna Carter Florence

A s a new teacher, one of the things I am learning this year is that *answering* questions may be hard, but *asking* a good question is even harder. When you make the transition from student to pastor or student to teacher, you stop thinking of the world in terms of exams that you have to pass, and you start imagining the world in terms of questions that might open it for someone else. A *good* question can start a good conversation; it can lead to amazing things. A *less-than-helpful* question is like running down a rabbit hole; it gets you nowhere. And if you want a classic example of a less-than-helpful question, it's right here, on the lips of the disciples, who, as usual, have a long way to go.

They were passing by a man who had been blind since birth. "Rabbi," the disciples ask, "who sinned, this man or his parents, that he was born blind?" Now, I know that doesn't look like such a bad question at first. This was an ancient culture which believed that illness was always somebody's fault. "Who sinned, this man or his parents?" That's a pretty good question for that culture. But it's not so off the wall for our culture either. We live in a litigation nation. We live in a talk-show society. We are very interested in the sins that create other people's misery and in figuring out who should have to pay for the damage. Pass a blind beggar on a street in Atlanta, and you might wonder, "Who's responsible for this situation? Who's at fault here?"—but it's no different from asking, "Who sinned?"

Who's to blame, Jesus, this man or his parents? What sin made him blind? Did his mother forget her prenatal vitamins? Did his father have a faulty gene? Did he grow up poor and malnourished and a victim of river blindness, because even though this disease is preventable, his country has no money for medical research and the rich Western nations won't forgive the debts of the developing nations? Did he take a new, experimental drug for AIDS that cost him his sight but prolonged his life, and was he willing to go blind just to buy a little more time, in case they discover a cure for this disease? Who sinned, Jesus? Who's to blame here?

When you're a pastor or a teacher or a rabbi such as Jesus, you have the prerogative, and I would even add the responsibility, to let your students know when they've asked the wrong question. It isn't about taking the student down a peg. It's about letting her know that if she goes down this rabbit hole, she is lost. That's what Jesus does. "Neither this man nor his parents sinned," he tells his disciples. "That's the wrong question. He was born blind so that God's works might be revealed in him."

When you're a disciple or a student of Christianity or the Bible, you have the prerogative, and I would even add the responsibility, to let your teachers and community know when you are struggling with what you see in the text. For me, a student at Jesus' feet, this is one of those times. I admit it. I am interested in *why* things happen; I am concerned about causes and accountability; and for me, this is not a satisfying exchange. Follow it to its logical conclusion, and you could face some pretty poor logic:

Ah—I see! It's nobody's fault that he's blind and poor and outcast. He was just born this way so that he could be a vessel for God's good works.

Ah—I see! It's nobody's fault that most of the people in this world are poor and struggling and oppressed, that human sin

*is epidemic and systemic, and that one nation's greed fuels the
misery of millions. These miserable people were just born that
way so they could be vessels for charity and development and
God's good works.*

*Ah—I see! Good news, and that should make everything
quiet on the western front tonight.*

That's one way to read it. But I don't think it gives Jesus much
credit. This isn't a story about accountability. It's a story about
blindness. This isn't a story about blaming the parents or the man
or Jesus or the Pharisees, or about deciding whether someone
broke the law or whether a person is worthy to speak for himself
or not. That's what the Pharisees think it's about; that's what the
parents think it's about; that's even what the disciples and the
man think it's about, before Jesus lets them know that they're
walking around in such a fog that they can't see their hands in
front of their faces. No, this is a story about being blind your
whole life, and then one day, having an encounter that opens
your eyes.

You know, every one of us sees things in a particular way. We
are blessed with the gift of perspective, which plants us down in
one place and lets us see the view from there. But it isn't always
what other people see. From where others stand, the view may
be slightly or even radically different, even when they share your
spot. Being blind literally means not seeing things that are
clearly visible to others around you. Being blind literally means
that when your neighbors describe the view from their place, you
don't get it. You physically don't get it! It isn't that you want to
disagree with them. You may even wish you could see their view.
But from where you stand, you physically can't.

We've heard a lot about blindness recently: literal blindness.
People have stood on both sides of what seems to be a question—what our church's response should be to gay and lesbian
people—and we have taken turns framing that question, but we
haven't always done a good job. To hear us tell it, this story
we're framing is about accountability and blame and upholding
the law and being worthy. It doesn't matter where we stand,

we're all thinking the same thing; we're all walking along with the disciples, clucking and shaking our heads and saying to one another:

> *Look at that person sitting over there, that blind person!*
>
> *Who sinned, that man or his parents, that he was born and raised that way?*
>
> *Who's responsible, this woman or her church, for making her read the Bible that way?*
>
> *Who's to blame, that man or his past, for making him so angry, so wounded, so judgmental?*
>
> *Who's at fault, that woman or her faith community, for letting her think that her behavior is acceptable?*

And then Jesus tells us that these are not the right questions. This blindness we see in everyone else is not a question of sin, theirs or that of the context they came from. It is not a question of blame or accountability. We *are blind so that God's works may be made known in us. We are blind so that God can encounter us and open our eyes.*

Let me repeat a story that I have heard some of you telling these last few weeks. I've heard people saying, "Once upon a time, I was in a place that seemed good and true to me. My parents and my church taught me to love, and they taught me the law, and I believed them with all my heart. I thought it was my responsibility to abide by the law. I thought it was my responsibility to hold people accountable for unworthy behavior. I didn't know you could be a Christian and look at it any other way. But then I met *you*, David, and you showed me how it looks from where you stand, and now the waters are muddy. Then I met *you*, Jean, and now I can't think about the law without thinking about your life. And I guess I must have been blind before, but I don't know what it means to see in this new way. I don't know if this sight is from God. If you are God's prophet to me, then how am I going to explain what happened to the people who knew me before?"

Do you know the amazing thing about this story? We can't

explain it, how we stop being blind about something. All we can say is it has to do with mud and meeting people.

Now, I know there must be cleaner ways to cure blindness. I don't relish the image of Jesus spitting in the dirt and mixing it up and smearing mud all over the guy's face. Not only is it gross, it's not even plausible! The Pharisees are so revolted that they can't believe the man would offer it as an explanation for how he received his sight; they keep asking him what happened, and he keeps repeating, "Look, I told you: he made mud, he put it on my eyes, then I washed, and now I see." He has to keep telling it, you know, because *it's never going to sound good.* It's never going to amount to a reasonable explanation for how a blind man could regain his sight. But that's how it really was, and is—right? You meet someone and life gets messy. You encounter the Christ and the mud, and the world looks different. It's bigger, holier, and you're so grateful for mud.

People are going to ask you about it: "So, tell us, what changed your mind? What made you see this issue differently? Tell us how you gained your sight!" You can't, not in a way that will satisfy anybody, because it has to do with mud and meeting people. But you know what? You don't have to explain. You don't have to talk about blame or accountability or behavior at all. Point them to this: " Look," you can say, "he put mud on my eyes, then I washed, and now I see. I was blind so that God's works could be revealed. I was blind so that I could meet you and know how glorious a thing it is to see with the eyes of another human being."

These are God's works. This is the light coming into the world. Thanks be to God.

Run the Risk

Mark 15:34

Brian K. Blount

He should have known it would happen. And yet, there in the darkness, his last breath of life gasping beyond his control, it seems to have come upon him suddenly, as though it were unexpected, as though he were caught unawares. It's a hard saying to understand, this cry of desperation offered up by a man whose usual public vocalizations were model words of faith and hope, even in hopeless situations. And yet there he was, crying out as though he were abandoned, as though he didn't understand it at all, as though the power and faith that had once stilled a storm and conquered death had now fled him. Christians across the ages have wondered what happened to him in that moment. He was the Son of God; he should have known. But there they are, those words: "My God, my God, why have *you* forsaken *me*?"

The book on this story is that Jesus was quoting from Psalm 22, and that it wasn't really a cry of desperation at all but a statement of hope even in the midst of great despair. That's because of the way Psalm 22 ends. Suddenly, inexplicably, the psalmist cries out, "I will praise you: You who fear the LORD, praise him!" (Ps. 22:22–23).

The gloom is gone. A feeling of celebration has grabbed its

111

place. But we don't know why. Things haven't changed. He doesn't say things have gotten better for him. It appears that he just *sees* things better.

But I have always been cautious of leading people past the despair to move too quickly into the hope of the psalm, especially where Jesus is concerned. Because I think it downplays the real and intense anguish of that opening line. I think Jesus did indeed feel pain and hurt, rejection and despair. That human side of him, the part that is so much like us, so much like the psalmist, felt the pain, knew the despair. I think we shouldn't look so quickly at the end of the psalm and make ourselves feel better, just because we want to believe, despite what Jesus said, despite the situation he was in, that he, too, really felt better than he sounded.

Christianity has become a "feel-good" religion. Too many people, I fear, look for it, come to it, become part of it, because they think it's supposed to make them feel better; not so much *do* better or *be* better but *feel* better.

That's one of the reasons Easter is such a great season. It's a feel-good, feel-better time. On the back side of a cross, hanging naked on a tree, exposed to the world, separated from God, lost from the hope of God's kingdom, we get colored eggs, snow-white bunnies, beautiful bonnets, and chocolate treats. It's hard to make somebody's death on a cross a feel-good thing. But we manage.

We feel better. We think, "Jesus really must have felt all right up there on that cross. He sounded distracted for a moment, but he was really quoting Psalm 22, and since, by the end of it, the psalmist was feeling good, Jesus must have been feeling good too."

We want so very badly for Christianity to make us feel good. Grace is like syrup: we want it warm and gooey and sticky, so that it not only makes us feel good when we see it and feel it on the outside, it makes us feel spiritually good, in God's good graces, on the inside. Deep inside our happy, good-feeling souls.

But to seek a Christianity that makes us feel good is to miss the powerful reality of what was happening to Jesus. And if we miss that, we also miss something special about ourselves.

Jesus was hanging up there on that cross because his faith wasn't a feel-good faith but a do-good and a be-good faith. He forgot about feelings and went about doing *too much* doing good. You've heard the expression "That guy's just *too* much." Jesus was going around doing way *too much.*

I'd say that too much going around changing things got Jesus in trouble. In Mark 14:58, Jesus is accused of saying that he would destroy the old temple and build a new one. Saying that, threatening to do that, he knew—he must have known—would cause all sorts of problems. You and I would know. If we went around challenging the way the world is run, the way schools are run, the way the church is run, challenging the people in power, we'd know, I think, that sooner or later we were going to get in trouble—because people don't like change, especially people in power, because it means they've got to give up some of that power when the changes come. And Jesus was talking about radical, dramatic, boundary-breaking change.

Think about that statement in 14:58. Jesus wasn't just talking about destroying the temple and rebuilding a new one in some future messianic sense. He had acted out his ministry as if he were a *present* threat to the temple. And we must remember that the temple for ancient Judaism was not the church of modern society. It wasn't open only for religious service on Sunday or midday prayer on Wednesday. It wasn't just a place for choir rehearsal or youth group meetings or bake sales and scout troops. It was the seat of social, political, and economic life in the Jewish community. It was the power base of Jewish life. It was the symbol of who these people were as a people. In short, it was the center of their lives, the place where their power, their being, *and* their beliefs were focused. And Jesus was perpetually at odds with this symbol because it represented life the way it was. Jesus represented life the way it could and should be.

In Jesus' time, if you were a Gentile you weren't even allowed in the temple, only in the outer courtyard. And if, God forbid, you were sick or lame or in some other health-related way unclean, you weren't even allowed on the premises. But Jesus challenged these restrictions. He foresaw a world where God was interested in all people, not just the men, not just the Jews, but a world where the men and women could worship as equals, a world where God's love was poured out upon Gentiles as well as Jews. He foresaw a world where those who were sick or lame, those who were lost or imprisoned, could enter and worship even though the leadership said they were unclean. That's what Jesus' life was about. He was about pulling to himself women and children and tax collectors and sinners and prisoners and lame and sick and blind and even the dead, all the people who were considered in some religious or political sense unclean, and he was saying that all this must change. But talking about this kind of change in a world that did not desire it meant trouble. It did not make people *feel* good. That's why Jesus was up there on that cross.

When we Christians today stop thinking "feel good" and concentrate on "do good" and "be good," what happened to Jesus will start happening to us. When we start talking about change, about redistributing power relationships in this world or this society or this church, then I think we all know that, sooner or later, people will get angry with us. Whatever your focus of change, whatever your desire to see this society do better, if you take on the challenge seriously, you take the chance of taking up and hanging on Jesus' cross. Challenge the way in which our government distributes its money and time, so that those who need the most care and financial attention in our society get it the least. Challenge our church about its efforts in urban ministry. Challenge our church to be more mission and less worship oriented. Challenge our politicians with the reality that we already have a society that takes care of people who can take care of themselves; proclaim that what we need instead is a society that protects those who are powerless, homeless, and hopeless. Challenge the very structure of how our society is organized, so that some people—blacks, women, Native Americans, Hispanics, and many other minorities—always seem to be losing ground. Take on those kinds of Jesus challenges in your own kind of risky, transformative discipleship. I wonder just how your efforts will be perceived by the powers in control. I don't think they'll like it. I don't think they'll appreciate you. I think they'll find some way to try to stop you.

And before you started doing all this, I think you'd know, and I'd know, that you were going to get yourself in trouble. So why on earth would you do it? Why would you *run the risk*?

I will always remember a college swimming class I took at eight o'clock on Monday, Wednesday, and Friday mornings. Most of us in the class already had some rudimentary swimming abilities; we had learned at places such as the Boy Scouts or community centers. It's just that we didn't really know how to swim well enough. But there was one woman there who'd had absolutely no previous swimming experience. This was her first attempt at water, and our instructor made us learn in the deep end.

He let us huddle around the edge of the pool at first. All of us held onto the sides, letting our feet dangle in the abyss. We were frightened at the depth; we shivered a bit from the cold; and we trembled when he walked up to us and told us to let go and move ourselves out into the middle and swim back. Pushing out there was easy; getting back was a little shakier. He stood there with a long stick in his hand, which he claimed would reach out to us in the water, so if we got in trouble we could latch onto it and be pulled to safety.

I remember that all of us tried it and did well—all of us until it was that woman's turn. He came up to her and touched her with the stick. He pointed to the depths, and he said, "Go." Dutifully, she obeyed. She pushed hard and ended up way out in the middle, too far to reach back to the side. She tried, though almost immediately she was in trouble. She reached, she screamed, she lunged. She was in deep, deep trouble.

Then she went down. When her head came back up the instructor, as he'd promised, had the stick right next to her. But she was in a panic now. She saw nothing but fear. She was scrambling. She thought she was dying. Some of us thought to move out to her, to help her, but the instructor ordered us to stay put.

"She won't ever learn if she can't face the fear, face up to it, and conquer it herself," he said. "Let her do it herself. If she wants to learn to swim," he said, "she must do it herself."

She did do it herself. She found the pole and she held on. But she hadn't learned to swim, so she had to do it again and again and again, and before she did learn, she panicked several more times. I always admired her when I saw her walk into the pool area on those early mornings. She could have found a way out of a swimming class. But instead of running, she faced the fear. Even knowing the prospects, even knowing what was in store for her on those early mornings, she knew she wanted to swim. So she did what she had to do in order to reach that goal: she faced the pain. She ran the risk of panic and going under because she believed the goal was worth it.

Sometimes, if you do what you know needs to be done, if you swim for God, if you swim through the hurt in order to reach God's people and their needs, then you also know you'll face a struggle. You know that sometimes you'll feel like sinking. And some of us won't think the struggle is worth it. We'll find a way to escape the challenge. One of my college roommates found a way: he had his family doctor write an excuse note; something about a chronic inner-ear infection, something about having a medical condition that meant he should be able to avoid a swimming class, to avoid the pushes out into the deep end.

Some of us Christians have our own kind of excuse notes. Let others do the mission; I'll put something in the offering plate. Let others shout and protest; I'll say amen. Let others stand up; I'll cheer from a distance. Let others try to feed the hungry; I'll donate canned food. Let others go into the inner city and try to build programs of change; I'll drop them off when they go in and pick them up when they're ready to come out.

But others know how important it is that God have swimmers, people who can survive the depths of hurt, the depths of fear, the depths of obstacles, and still reach out to God's people. These are the people who run the risk of swimming for God in turbulent political, religious, social, and personal seas. Are you one of them?

What I'm trying to say is that Christianity is about risk, not about feeling good. It is about making changes in our lives the same way Jesus risked making changes in the lives of all those who lived around him. From where he stood on the shore of salvation, he saw that we were in trouble out here on our ocean of problems and oppressions. Jesus saw that we were in too much of a mess, that nothing less than a monumental ministry dedicated to transforming the oppressive traditions of his people would save us. That's why he risked the kind of ministry Mark records throughout the pages of his Gospel. Like that young lady in my college days, Jesus pushed off into the deep end of human misery and oppression with the goal of making radical changes. Come the garden of Gethsemane, I figure he realized finally that his head was underwater. But I think he knew from the start that he was going to go under. And yet he did it anyway. He ran the risk because he knew that the gift of his transformative ministry was worth the price he'd have to pay to give it.

We should know that if we try to live up to what Christianity is all about, we will come to those moments in life when we will also feel despair. We'll feel like we're going under. And in those times, some of us will wonder if learning to swim for God is worth the price we have to pay. Jesus wondered: "My God, my God, why have you forsaken me?"

If he wondered, we all will.

Perhaps somewhere in your heart, deep in the recesses of your spirit, God is calling, or perhaps God already has called you to change something in your life or in the life of someone around you. Maybe it's something small in your own life, your family, your marriage, your job. Or maybe it's something large, such as your community, your state, your profession, maybe even your very life; maybe even your church. Maybe God is telling you in some way that following him isn't just about feeling good. Maybe somewhere in your heart you hear a voice suggesting that you *do* some good somewhere. If you answer, more than likely you'll take a risk. It may be something as small as giving up a Saturday afternoon to do a mission project. It may be something as large as giving up your own dreams to take on God's dreams. I can't tell you to follow that voice; no one could. I can only tell you that when God calls, it's always a risk when you answer.

You know, the phone company has a service: Caller ID. There is a little screen that attaches to your phone, and when the phone rings, the screen displays the phone number of the person calling you. Sometimes I think that if our life phones rang into our consciousness, and we looked on a little screen and it said, "God," "God is calling," some of us might not want to pick up, might not want to know what it is God wants. God wants too much change from us most of the time.

I know that answering God will put you in darkness sometimes; it'll get you lost sometimes; it'll get you hurt sometimes; but always, it'll get you where God wants you to be, and perhaps where someone or some people in trouble desperately need you to be. That's where the good news, the grace, is in the Gospel of Mark. The good news, the grace of God's imminent kingdom, doesn't just come to you. *You* are the good news that God is sending out to others. *You* are the grace that does whatever it takes to transform their lives, even when you know that the boundary-breaking transformation you attempt may inevitably invite your own destruction. But God's grace can make changes in our world; that's why God extends it. That's why God sends you. You are, by your boundary-breaking kingdom discipleship, the living representation of God's heavenly grace. That's why you run the risk. It's why Jesus ran it. Because when you run Jesus' kind of transformative risk, you are running for God.

PART 4

Living by
Scripture

Scripture

The Word of Life

W. Eugene March

*The Supreme Judge, by which all controversies of religion
are to be determined, and all decrees of councils, opinions
of ancient writers, doctrines of men, and private spirits,
are to be examined, and in whose sentence we are to rest,
can be no other but the Holy Spirit speaking in the
Scripture.*[1]

The authority of scripture in the church is almost universally
accepted. Some people lean almost exclusively on one
Testament or the other or on only a few books in the Bible,
rather than on most of the canon; nonetheless, the authority of
scripture is not directly challenged. Christians largely accept the
church's teaching that believers are to live in some way under
the authority of scripture.

The "in some way" is the issue! How does the Holy Spirit
"speak" in scripture? What is the role of the community? What
is the place of individual conscience? How can technical knowledge of the biblical languages and of the background and circumstances of the writing of the Bible best be used in the
church? How do modern Christians find God's word of life in
the reading and interpretation of an ancient book? These are a

few of the questions that prompt this reflection on "Scripture: The Word of Life."

The Place of Community

Communities of believers have been integral to creating "scripture" and living by it for several thousand years. Insofar as research can determine, communities preserved the words of persons believed to be under the power of God's Spirit. These communities then studied and respected these words as part of the common life. Then, and only then, after hundreds of years, a canon—scripture—was announced and confirmed by the church in its councils.

For the Old Testament, several communities can be detected within the Bible itself. Some groups preserved and shared the work of the prophets. Accounts of Israel's escape and wilderness wanderings were preserved, circulated orally and then in writing. Liturgical and legal materials, first collected at various holy places, were gathered. Genealogical records, astrological records, collections of proverbial sayings, and the like were developed. Narratives emerged as people recounted their various experiences of God's graciousness.

The earliest centuries of this process of collecting and arranging the manifold fruits of God's Spirit can be sketched only vaguely. But by the end of the Babylonian exile (ca. 500 before the Common Era), something like the Pentateuch or the Torah, the first five books of our Bible, was being used by communities in Babylon as well as Palestine and even in Egypt. Next followed the completion of the collection of the prophetic traditions, and later still the materials found in Chronicles, Ezra, Nehemiah, Psalms, Proverbs, Job, and other "wisdom" books.

By the time of Jesus, the "law and the prophets," that is, the Torah (Pentateuch) and the Former Prophets (Joshua–Kings) and Latter Prophets (Isaiah, Jeremiah, Ezekiel, and the twelve "Minor Prophets"), were "authoritative." No official action had been taken that made these books "scripture." Rather, community use of and respect for these writings gave them their power.

Theologically speaking, the Holy Spirit working within communities of believers enlivened these particular writings.

Only after the destruction of Jerusalem by the Romans in 70 of the Common Era did a group of survivors act to fashion a "canon." This took place over several decades in a community at Jamnia (Jabne) in the Galilee and marked the beginning of what is now known as Judaism. For several centuries to follow, in several different locales, Jewish scholars pondered the words of their canon, their scripture (which included all thirty-nine books of the "Protestant Old Testament"), and created many volumes of interpretation called the Talmud.

For Christians, the process was similar but took only about half as long. Paul's letters were, apparently, among the first documents collected and shared among the churches with which he was involved. Further, different communities in Palestine and across the Mediterranean area began to use "gospels" written in their midst and in tune with their circumstances. By the end of the first century C.E., almost all of the writings that came to form the Christian canon, scripture, were being used extensively among the churches.

As with the Jewish canon, use came before official recognition. The canon of the New Testament was not officially created by the church until the fourth century C.E., but in fact, with regard to use of and respect for the documents, the process—including the acceptance of the Old Testament as scripture—was well on the way toward completion by the end of the second century C.E.[2]

It is instructive to recognize the authority derived from community use. The reputation of Paul no doubt helped get his letters an initial hearing, but it was their quality and usefulness that got them a second reading. There were many Gospels written, but only four received wide enough usage to gain them a place in the canon of scripture later officially adopted. The same process was true for the New Testament as for what we now know as the Old Testament: only centuries after the initial writing and reception by the community were questions of authorship debated and linked with the issue of authority. In other words, use by and among communities of believers made these documents "scripture." The Spirit actively worked through these particular books for the nurture of the communities that held them dear. Theories of inspiration and declarations by church councils rightly followed but were expounded only centuries later, to help us understand what had happened and why.

As the contemporary church struggles to find and hear a word of life in scripture, the biggest single obstacle is ignorance. Most North American Christians simply do not know the Bible well enough to be influenced by its perspective. Children may get some introduction to some parts of the Bible, but this is incomplete for most. Adults with very little knowledge are reduced to trying to make sense of a Bible presented in bits and pieces through the preaching ministry but seldom are engaged in serious, ongoing study.

There are many reasons that such is the case today within the churches. High mobility, extreme individualism, apparent relativism among value systems—such factors work against people gaining a thorough knowledge of the Old and New Testaments. There is so much to do and so little time to do it in that, for all too many, Bible study simply does not make the "must-do" list. I have not known a congregation that did not put adult education high on its priority list, but I also have seen very few that actually followed through and created the kind of community where becoming well acquainted with the Bible was prized and actually happened.

If communities of believers have historically been crucial for the Bible to become a source of instruction and inspiration, then the breakdown of the community evidenced in many churches is a serious issue. Life together around scripture does not seem to be taking place widely. Large numbers of individual adult church members seem to see little reason to spend the time and effort required to know the Bible. If the community does not live in such a way as to insist on the importance of this enterprise, it will not happen. To live by scripture requires the serious commitment of the church community in order to enlist the interest and effort of the overscheduled, underprepared adults who fill our churches.

Why is all this talk about community important? Because Presbyterians and Reformed Christians, at least, believe that the Holy Spirit works primarily through the church gathered in community. Of course, the Spirit's work is not limited to gatherings of believers, but on matters of policy and practice, the action of the community under the direction of the Holy Spirit is critical. But if we are to be led by the scriptures, the inspired words of individuals gathered and preserved by communities under the guidance of the Spirit, then we have to *know the scriptures*. This knowledge needs to be thorough, not just piecemeal. The Bible must color the very way in which we perceive reality, not merely be another source among others quoted to one's advantage.

Only the community, with the Spirit's aid, can inspire a serious dedication to learning and hold accountable those who presume to declare God's will to the gathering. Individual conscience is certainly important (particularly to the dissenter), but finally, the church moves ahead by community decisions under the discipline of God's Holy Spirit. Biblically informed and sensitive individuals, speaking their consciences, are essential if the community is to hear God's Word. Debate is inevitable and healthy. Full agreement with one another on every biblical passage is unlikely and unnecessary. But the community of believers is the proper setting in which interpretations of scripture will shape faith and action.

The Task of Interpretation

What does it take to become biblically literate in order to live by scripture? We affirm that all have access to scripture with no requirement of any clerical intermediary. But just because all are free and encouraged to study scripture does not mean that all are equally qualified as interpreters. The task of Bible study, when done seriously, is not easy. In our age of instant gratification, such news will not be received happily, but it is nonetheless the case. There is a clear path to follow if one is willing to make the effort.

First, there is the Bible itself, all sixty-six books. It is probably not best to start with Genesis and read to Revelation. Rather, a study plan should be developed that allows one to survey the whole Bible in an organized, steady, thoughtful manner. The temptation will be to read books about the Bible rather than the Bible itself, but the goal is to become as familiar with the Bible as with one's favorite sports club or novel or motion picture or musical group. Only by reading and rereading can such familiarity be achieved. Longtime readers of the Bible acquire an awareness of, among other things, idioms, images, themes, and conflicting claims that facilitate understanding and encourage the ongoing quest to hear God's word of life.[3]

If one is bold enough and determined enough, one will make an effort to learn at least some Hebrew and Greek, the major languages in which the Bible first was written. Obviously, this cannot be done overnight, but some facility can be achieved more quickly than one might imagine. Most of us do not like the idea of learning another language, but there are some aspects of the text that simply cannot be translated. To know the Bible thoroughly in English is good. To read some Hebrew and Greek, at least, is even better.

Unfortunately, few people will commit themselves to the discipline required to learn the biblical language. The next best thing is to study at least two or three English translations and, perhaps, one in Spanish, French, or German, as one is able. It is best to choose one translation and become very familiar with the scripture through that text but then check it occasionally by studying other translations.

Somewhere along the way, questions will arise as to the meaning of particular terms, the geographical location of sites, the historical situation to which a writer refers, and so forth. Footnotes in some Bibles may help. Dictionaries of the Bible can provide helpful information. Commentaries and books of interpretation will offer varied suggestions concerning meaning. Such background material is very useful, but remember, it is a supplement, not a replacement, for studying scripture itself.[4]

By now, the scope of the project of biblical literacy should be clear. This is not something that can be done overnight; nor can it be done alone. Individuals need the discipline, encouragement, and correction of others in the quest to know and understand the Bible more fully. This is a lifelong quest to which we are challenged. The church has long insisted that scripture can open the word of life to us. If so, then the Bible is well worth getting to know, and getting to know well.

But the need to interpret does not wait until one is thoroughly versed in the Bible. Life is never that neat. Christians at every stage of their lives have to make decisions and choices. The Bible is a major guide to how we are to live, how we are to decide what is God's way and what is not, and how we are to act. Life does not wait until we are fully prepared. So what do we do as we continue on our path of gaining awareness and understanding of the word of life?

There are several guidelines that the Reformed tradition has long recognized as helpful. First, try your best to know what the plain sense of the biblical passage is. Consider the style of writing (a psalm is not the same as a parable, for instance), the literary context in which the passage is situated, and the historical situation in which it was written. Do not take things out of context, and do not too quickly interpret a plain word in a figurative sense. For instance, to interpret the snake in Genesis 3 as the figure of the devil, which developed in postbiblical times, is to ignore the plain meaning of the text.

Next, when interpreting a text that is unclear—one whose plain sense is difficult to determine—you should go to passages that are clearer. The principle is to let scripture interpret scripture. Many Christians have taken isolated and unclear texts (e.g., Matt. 24:30–31; 1 Thess. 4:16–17) and have developed an elaborate theory about a "rapture" where Christians will be plucked up out of the world at the end of time. A much clearer text reminds us that we simply cannot know about such matters and should therefore avoid speculation (e.g., Matt. 24:3-44; Mark 13:32–37; Luke 17:23–24; 21:20– 24). Obscure texts thought pertinent to a wide variety of other issues (even sexuality) have been equally misused.

While working with the plain sense of a passage and using scripture to read scripture, we also need to remember what scripture is and is not. The Bible is not a scientific textbook or a book of magic. The Bible is neither a blueprint to the future nor a book of answers for all of life's questions. The subject of the Bible is God and God's way, God's deliverance, God's continuing care and direction. How God relates to humankind is at the heart of scripture; theories about the expanding universe and the social construction of gender are not.

Finally, when interpreting texts, an overarching principle is the centrality of Jesus Christ. For Christians, it is in Jesus Christ that God most clearly defines the relationship of God and human beings. Interpretations of the Bible that forget, ignore, or deviate from the witness of the Bible to Jesus Christ are inadequate at best and destructive at worst. God's love incarnate in Jesus of Nazareth should be a guiding light in the process of understanding and interpreting particular passages. It is inconceivable in light of Jesus' life, death, and resurrection to believe that we are supposed to hate, abuse, or kill one another. The centrality of Christ in the church and in the Bible prohibits such interpretation.

Love for and respect for one another is cardinal when Jesus Christ is at the center of our common life. By God's Spirit, in the course of the twentieth century, the Presbyterian Church has been led to a reconsideration of its teaching concerning divorce and its view of the role of women in the church. In each instance, biblical passages could be found that seemed to support previous practice. Nonetheless, the community, with its eye on the teachings of the Lord Jesus Christ, moved in a decidedly new direction.

The task of interpretation is not easy and should not be taken lightly. Lifelong preparation that includes hard study of the Bible as a literary document that has a human context and historical setting is required. Responsible interpretation requires seeking the plain sense of a text, letting scripture interpret scripture, remembering what scripture is and is not, and keeping one's eyes fixed on the Lord of life, Jesus Christ.[5]

Preparation also includes a dedication to prayer, and with it a "devotional" reading of scripture. Individuals and groups can submit to the shaping power of God's Spirit most readily by reading and reflecting on scripture. Devotional reading, like serious study of the Bible, is in itself a type of prayer. It should be at the heart of our spirituality. This has been the witness of the church for centuries, and we should take heed.

All our study, discussion, reflection, and prayer, as individuals and within groups, must finally be tested by the larger community under the discipline of God's Holy Spirit. Debate and controversy are inevitable when important issues are under consideration. The Bible is not a handbook of proof texts to be slammed on the heads of opponents. It is a common source of guidance and inspiration, a witness to God and Jesus Christ, a place where we can meet God and be given encouragement, support, and, sometimes, surprising new direction.

The Word of Life

All that has been described thus far is to encourage a turning to the Bible for those who wish to receive God's word of life. Whether or not there are other sources for discerning God is not under consideration here. Centuries of experience in the church testify that the reading and study of the Bible is the most reliable place wherein Christians can anticipate being addressed by the living Word, the Lord Jesus Christ. Thus, the desire to hear God's word of life should draw one to the Bible.

Ezekiel 18 presents a thoughtful reflection on the problem of individual sin and punishment. In the course of the prophet's review, there is a description of what life in God's way entails. Such a life is marked by devotion to God (no idolatry), respect for others, honesty, justice, compassion, and care, in both private and community life (see Ezek. 18:5–9 as contrasted with Ezek. 18:10–13). The passage concludes with these moving words: "Cast away from you all the transgressions that you have committed against me, and get yourselves a new heart and a new spirit! Why will you die, O house of Israel? For I have no pleasure in the death of anyone, says the Lord GOD. Turn, then, and live" (Ezek. 18:31–32).

God's commandments provide guidance to abundant living. The Ten Commandments, for instance, while expressed negatively, describe a community where people show respect for God and for one another (Ex. 20:1–17; Deut. 5:6–21). Jesus is remembered as summing up the commandments with references to Deuteronomy and Leviticus by saying: " 'You shall love the Lord your God with all your heart, and with all your soul, and with all your mind.' This is the greatest and first commandment. And a second is like it: 'You shall love your neighbor as yourself.' On these two commandments hang all the law and the prophets" (Matt. 22:37–40; cf. Lev. 19:18b; Deut. 6:45; Luke 10:25–28). Jesus also is remembered for giving but one commandment: "Just as I have loved you, you also should love one another" (John 13:34). This kind of love was radical, embracing even—especially—"enemies" (cf. Matt. 5:33–45; Luke 6:27–36). For the apostle Paul, this was possible only by the power of the Spirit. He described the fruit of the Spirit as "love, joy, peace, patience, kindness, generosity, faithfulness, gentleness, and self-control. There is no law against such things" (Gal. 5:22–23). All are in keeping with the attitudes enjoined in and the results of living by God's commandments.

The Bible provides rich instruction and guidance about how individuals and communities should structure their lives. Many of the commandments and teachings may not seem "workable" or "appropriate" in contemporary North American society. Ours is not primarily an agricultural, village-based community. Many aspects of modern life were not even imagined, much less addressed. Nonetheless, with the Spirit's help, the Bible continues to challenge, correct, and encourage those who will attend to it with devotion and diligence.

Further, the Bible itself assures us that God's ways are not our ways (e.g., Isa. 55:8; Rom. 11:33). Utterly new and unexpected things may come as God chooses (e.g., Isa. 48:6–8). The word of God brings new life, even resurrection! Dividing walls of hostility can and have been, surprisingly, broken down (Eph. 2:14–15). There are things clearly unpleasing to God, but the good news is that, nevertheless, God is "merciful and gracious, slow to anger, and abounding in steadfast love" (Ex. 34:6–7; cf. Ps. 103:8–10; Joel 2:13; Jonah 4:2). Both the incredible mercy and the willingness to do new things were incarnate in Jesus of Nazareth in his ministry to the outcasts of his society and to all the disinherited. Where may we next be led? The ways of God are not our ways, thank God!

But the challenge and the gift are that our ways may become more like God's. Scripture offers us ample instruction as to what God desires. Stories of boldness and courage are to be found there; proverbial sayings that encapsulate wisdom wrung from experience; visions of what might be, and laments over missed opportunities; cries of anguish provoked by tragedy. All are contained in the Bible and are offered as guides in our quest for life. We cannot get there alone, but by God's grace, empowered by God's Spirit, it really can happen.

For nearly three decades, church membership in the "mainline" churches in North America has been declining. A number of sociological and ecclesiastical factors can be cited to "explain" this decline.[6] During this period, biblical literacy also has declined significantly (at least, if the degree of biblical knowledge among candidates for ministry entering our seminaries is a trustworthy measure). Thus, as the churches have faced significant issues, not the least of which is the issue of decline, they have been ill equipped with respect to biblical knowledge or even biblical familiarity. Too many with insufficient knowledge of the Bible and inadequate systems of interpretation have been trying to tell others what to think and what to do, and the larger community is not well equipped to engage issues biblically or theologically in a responsible manner. Efforts often are sincere, but ignorance abounds.

God continues to offer the word of life through the scripture. The pain and suffering of humanity bring sorrow to God. The church is challenged to join in Jesus' ministry as he described it, using Isaiah's words: "The Spirit of the Lord is upon me . . . to bring good news to the poor. He has sent me . . . to proclaim the year of the Lord's favor" (Luke 4:18–19; cf. Isa. 61:1–4). God does not desire the death of anyone. New life, abundant life, is God's aim.

Whether the church—whether we—will seriously seek God's

Word of life is yet to be seen. The use of the Bible in recent years, when it has occurred at all, has too often been unhelpful. Pulling six or eight obscure verses out of the whole Bible to "justify" any ecclesiastical policy is potentially harmful. Why? Because it approaches the Bible in what seems to be a literalistic and legalistic manner, which the Bible itself rejects. When we "proof-text," we suggest to the uninformed that Bible study is mainly important to "prove" points. Too often texts have been arranged "for" and "against" issues, irrespective of their biblical context, their plain sense, or the centrality of Christ. Such uses of the Bible are not useful in bringing the church into a living engagement with scripture. And such an engagement is what is desperately needed to help resolve some of the deep differences among us.

The tasks before us are difficult. To educate and sensitize a new generation to the context and use of the Bible will not be easy. But if we are to be true to our calling, the effort must be made. Individual Christians, to say nothing of the church gathered, need the refreshing, invigorating, challenging word of life that God offers by the power of the Spirit through the scripture. There are signs of awakening, a renewal. We need a new set of eyeglasses to see what God is doing. They are waiting for us in scripture, God's Word of Life.

NOTES

1. "The Westminster Confession of Faith," chap. 1, 10, *Book of Confessions*, 6.010.
2. For a much more detailed discussion of the canonical process, see D. N. Freeman, "Canon of the Old Testament," and A. C. Sandberg, "Canon of the New Testament," in *The Interpreter's Dictionary of the Bible,* supplementary volume (Nashville: Abingdon Press, 1976), 130–140; Phyllis A. Bird, "The Authority of the Bible," in *The New Interpreter's Bible* (Nashville: Abingdon Press, 1994–), 1:33–49.
3. Celia Brewer Marshall, in *A Guide through the Old Testament* and *A Guide through the New Testament* (Louisville, Ky.: Westminster/John Knox Press, 1989 and 1994), provides helpful guides to mastering the content of the Bible through self-directed study.

4. There are a number of useful introductory articles that will help give orientation and background for a study of the Bible in *The New Interpreter's Bible* (Nashville: Abingdon Press, 1994–), vols. 1 and 8.
5. See *Presbyterian Understanding and Use of the Holy Scripture,* a position statement of the General Assembly of the Presbyterian Church (U.S.A.), available through Presbyterian Distribution Service, #OGA-92-003.
6. For a thorough discussion, see the seven-volume series, The Presbyterian Presence, ed. Milton J Coalter, John M. Mulder, and Louis B. Weeks (Louisville, Ky.: Westminster/John Knox Press, 1990–1992), and also the conclusions drawn from their research in their book *Vital Signs: The Promise of Mainstream Protestantism* (Grand Rapids: Wm. B. Eerdmans Publishing Co., 1996).

Reading the Bible
and Reflecting on History

Jack Rogers

W e can know God! That is good news. The Bible, Holy
Scripture, is the "ordinary means" by which we know
God, who is revealed in Jesus Christ.[1] It is very important, therefore, that we understand the kind of knowledge that we have in
scripture and how it comes to us.

Practical and Theoretical Knowledge

I have made my living during most of my adult life teaching
both philosophy and theology. I have always been fascinated by
Plato and Aristotle as well as by Paul and Augustine. Insights
gained in one field often illumine the other. We humans also
tend to cross-reference and sometimes confuse the two.

The Westminster Confession in its initial chapter, "Of the
Holy Scripture," immediately raises issues both biblical and
philosophical: "Although the light of nature, and works of creation and providence, do so far manifest the goodness, wisdom
and power of God, as to leave men inexcusable; yet are they not
sufficient to give that knowledge of God, and of his will, which is
necessary unto salvation." If the light in human nature and on

God's creation is not sufficient to provide a saving knowledge of God, what is? According to Westminster, that makes "the Holy Scripture to be most necessary."[2]

Biblically, the passage quoted above sounds like a direct echo of Paul in Romans 1. I often ask my students to read Rom. 1:18–20 and then ask them two questions. The first is a practical, theological question: What is the point of this passage? If you were going to preach a sermon on it, what would you want people to take home with them? The practical point is pretty clear: everyone knows God, and therefore all are without excuse. No one is innocent. All of us are sinners because we have not lived up to the knowledge of God that we have.

Then I ask them a theoretical, philosophical question: *How* do we know God? Then the fun begins. Some argue strongly that God is known directly in the human mind and heart. Others assert just as energetically that God is known by observing nature, God's creation. After we have worked on it a while, I interject that this theoretical, philosophical question cannot be answered by this biblical text. It depends on where you choose to put the emphasis. Both answers are possible. Philosophically, if you are a Platonist and believe that reality is known directly by the mind, you will choose the first option. If you are an Aristotelian and believe that all knowledge comes through the human senses—sight, hearing, taste, touch, and smell—you will opt for the second choice.

Calvin (and the Westminster Confession), following Plato and Augustine, believed that God impressed the knowledge of God's person and presence directly on our hearts. Calvin's medieval Roman Catholic opponents followed Aristotle and Thomas Aquinas and asserted that we could know God by observing nature and reasoning back to God as a first cause. They disagreed on the theoretical question because they were informed by different philosophical schools of thought. But they fully agreed on the practical, biblical issue: all people know God and are without excuse if they do not worship and serve God.[3]

Salvation and Service

In this simple exercise we have learned a valuable lesson. Scripture does not tell us everything we want to know. The Bible tells us what we need to know! What do we most need to know? The Westminster Confession of Faith speaks of "those things which are necessary to be known, believed, and observed, for salvation."[4] In another place it points us to all things necessary for God's "glory, man's salvation, faith, and life."[5] What we need to know from scripture is how to be rightly related to God and to other people. That should not surprise us, since Jesus said that the whole law was summed up in the two commandments to love God and to love our neighbor.

Our Reformed theological tradition is emphatic that scripture has a twofold purpose: (1) to bring us to salvation in Jesus Christ and (2) to guide us in living a life of Christian faith.[6] The Bible, therefore, is a book with a practical purpose. It gives us what the early church theologians called *sapientia*, "divine wisdom," as opposed to *scientia*, "science," or the knowledge of temporal things.[7] The classical text on the authority of the Bible, 2 Tim. 3:16–17, points to a practical rather than theoretical purpose for scripture. It speaks of the *usefulness* of the Bible: "All scripture is inspired by God and is useful for teaching, for reproof, for correction, and for training in righteousness, so that everyone who belongs to God may be proficient, equipped for every good work."

Controversies of Religion

There is an additional consideration. According to the Westminster Confession, the first purpose of scripture, to lead us to salvation, is clear. The second purpose, to guide us in living the Christian life, is not always so clear. The confession says, "All things in scripture are not alike plain in themselves, nor alike clear unto all." That we know from experience. Those things essential to salvation, however, are "so clearly propounded and opened in some place of Scripture or other, that not only the learned, but the unlearned, in a due use of the ordinary means, may attain unto a sufficient understanding of them."[8] That is a seventeenth-century way of saying that if you go to church, hear the scripture read, and listen to the preacher expound its basic message, the Holy Spirit will enable you to get the point.

When we try to apply the scripture to every question we encounter in life, things get a bit murkier. The Westminster Confession indicates that we will experience "controversies of religion."[9] Generally, things become controversial precisely because scripture does not address or give a completely clear account of them. Now, some people may think that the scripture is quite clear on a given point. Others may also think that the scripture is clear but that it gives a different answer. That is how controversy starts.

What do we do when we have a controversy among Christian people over what they think is a religious issue? The Westminster Confession says: go study the Hebrew and Greek text![10] That is a way of saying that neither raising our voices nor saying our prayers is sufficient in itself to solve the problem. What we had better do is study the matter and be patient and tolerant with one another. It is because the authority of scripture is so precious to us, and because we want so deeply to be faithful to it, that we sometimes get into such awful arguments.

The problem is not with scripture. It is with us. We are sometimes asking the Bible to answer a question it was never meant to address. Other times we are so convinced by our culture that something is perfectly clear that we are unable to see that the Bible has a very different slant on the matter. That brings us to the other critical factor in the knowing process, namely, what we bring to the text.

Adequate but Not Absolute Knowledge

As the apostle Paul says in 1 Cor. 13:12, "we see in a mirror, dimly." Only when we are finally in the direct presence of God will we see face to face. Until then, human knowledge is indirect, like seeing in a mirror. Human knowledge is adequate but not absolute. Our knowledge of the world and of God is limited, partial, but adequate for our human needs. That knowledge is sufficient for salvation, right relationship to God. That knowledge also points us in the direction of service, right relationship to our neighbor.

The biblical witness to God's will for our lives is adequate but not obvious. The Bible always needs to be interpreted. We all interpret. We all come to the Bible with glasses that bring the biblical material into a focus of application to our time and situation. The Bible doesn't need to change. But sometimes the focus of our glasses needs to change. We sometimes need new lenses.

A Culturally Shaped Worldview

What blurs our vision? What keeps us from seeing what God is saying to us in scripture? There may be many things. One of the principal ones is that the glasses through which we view reality are shaped by our culture.

Culture is the complete nonbiologically transmitted heritage of the human race. We are in culture as fish are in water. We may be more or less aware of it, but we cannot escape it. Our culture fashions the unconsciously accepted glasses through which we view our environment. The result is a worldview that enables us to interpret the reality in which we live.[11]

Each of us has a worldview, which is not peculiar to us. We learn it from our culture. It is a comprehensive, mostly subconscious perspective on reality. A worldview is a set of assumptions about reality shared by a community of people. It tells us what is normal, valuable, and virtuous. Without a culture, we could not function in society. We would have to investigate each new experience at length instead of knowing reflexively how we ought to respond.

When we move from one nation to another or from one ethnic subculture to another, we quickly become aware of our own worldview. I remember talking to an international student who had just arrived from Africa. I asked him, "Was your family able to come with you?" He answered, "No, only my wife and children." For me the answer would have been yes. My culture has taught me to call the nuclear family of husband, wife, and children a family. But for my African friend, family was an extended group of relatives far beyond the nuclear family.

My wife and I lived for five years in The Netherlands while I was studying for my doctorate. We became close friends with a couple old enough to have been our parents. They were conservative Christian people. When discussing the presidential elections in the United States, we were surprised to discover that they found it hard to believe that any Christian could be a Republican. In their culture, it was assumed that the Christian attitude toward, for example, health care was that the government should provide it at little or no cost to everyone. What Americans would call socialism to them was simply the application of the Christian gospel. That is what their culture had taught them.

What has our culture taught us? Might our culturally shaped glasses be blurring our vision of the gospel? It is very difficult to look at our own glasses. They are too close to us. We can, however, look at our history and become aware of how American culture has in the past blurred Christians' views of the gospel.

Slavery and Segregation

Two instances in which American culture blurred our vision of the gospel were our acceptance of slavery for African Americans and the subordination of women to men. We need painfully to remember that virtually all Christian people at one time believed that the Bible sanctioned slavery and that women were intended by God to remain forever subjected to men. They were as sure that they were submitting to biblical authority and that they understood the Bible correctly as we ever have been. It should give us pause regarding our certainties.

The first pronouncement of Presbyterians regarding slavery was by the Synod of New York and Philadelphia in 1787. Its stance was definitive for over half a century. While declaring that, as Americans, we were for the principle of universal liberty, it stated that this could not be applied to slaves. Why? Our culture had taught us, and Presbyterians uncritically accepted, the notion that slaves were "dangerous." Thus the church recommended "prudent measures," consistent with the interests of (white) society, that might lead to the eventual abolition of slavery.[12]

In 1818 the Presbyterian General Assembly made what was later considered a brave statement against slavery. It sympathized with slaveholders, however, who, it declared, were not responsible for this evil. Why? Christians accepted the general cultural view of slaves, "their ignorance and their vicious habits generally."[13] More than forty years later, the Presbyterian Church in the Confederate States of America reinforced the cultural prejudice against African Americans, saying, "As long as that race, in its comparative degradation co-exists, side by side, with the white, bondage is its normal condition."[14]

James Henley Thornwell, a leading architect of the Presbyterian attitude toward slavery, evidences how thoroughly his culture controlled his view of scripture. He wrote that "if men had drawn their conclusions upon this subject only from the Bible, it would no more have entered into any human head to denounce slavery as a sin, than to denounce monarchy, aristocracy or poverty."[15] Thornwell's successor as the formative Presbyterian theologian in the South, Robert Lewis Dabney, as late as 1888 was still defending slavery. He argued that it was a radical social theory that would assert "all men are born free and equal." That, according to Dabney, was "an attack on God's Word."[16]

Eventually nearly all Presbyterians came to see that it was not Christ but culture that sanctioned slavery and segregation. Difficult as it is to admit that we have been wrong, a report by the Presbyterian Church in the United States (PCUS) in 1956 stated, "We no longer argue that human slavery is justified by the Bible, and in accord with God's will. Some of our grandfathers did so argue, declaring that slavery was God's permanent institution. Through the illumination of the Holy Spirit, we have come to a different understanding on this subject. We see that the Bible passages they quoted were not kept by them in the larger context of the Bible as a whole."[17]

The context of the Bible as a whole includes an awareness of the cultural limitations of people in other times and cultures. We cannot argue that because slavery was practiced in the Bible that it is justified now. Preeminently, that larger context means looking at all of scripture through the lens of Jesus' life and ministry. It was Jesus who made outcasts such as the Samaritan the heroes of his parables, rather than writing them off as ignorant and dangerous, as he had been taught by his culture.

A theological shift was made explicit in 1976 when the PCUS General Assembly adopted "A Declaration of Faith." On race it stated, "The antagonisms between races, nations and neighbors are manifestations of our sin against God."[18] Regarding the interpretation of scripture, "A Declaration of Faith" affirmed, "When we encounter apparent tensions and conflicts in what Scripture teaches us to believe and do, the final appeal must be to the authority of Christ."[19]

Subordination of Women

In 1811 the Presbyterian General Assembly first officially acknowledged women's significant contribution through voluntary organizations for missions, benevolence, and social reform. The men of the Assembly announced, "Benevolence is always attractive, but when dressed in female form [it] possesses peculiar charms."[20] That same year a Presbyterian minister put forth the culturally accepted view of women in a typically patronizing manner: "Who will not delight in the sweet and heavenly work of honoring the weaker vessels, and of endeavoring to make them ornamental and useful in the house of God."[21]

This concept of "ornamental womanhood" expressed the pervasive cultural view that women could practice their piety in private, but the public realm was for men alone. As with slavery, Presbyterians in the nineteenth-century defended the status quo that prohibited women, among other things, from voting or owning property. Men selected proof texts from the Bible that described the cultural role of women in the ancient Near Eastern culture and used them to justify their own subordination of women.

We forget how passionately leading Presbyterian theologians felt they were defending the Bible by rejecting women's rights. Charles Hodge, in a negative review of a book that attacked slavery, justified slavery by the analogy of the necessary subordination of women. He wrote, "If women are to be emancipated from subjection to the law which God has imposed upon them; . . . if, in studied insult to the authority of God we are to renounce, in the marriage contract, all claim to obedience, . . . there is no deformity of human character from which we turn with deeper loathing than from a woman forgetful of her nature and clamorous for the vocations and rights of men."[22]

Change came very gradually. In 1916, the PCUS General Assembly continued to forbid women to preach or to be ordained but left open the possibility that women could speak and lead in prayer in the local congregational prayer meeting. That possibility was enough to cause sixty-one commissioners to protest that this would be a violation of biblical authority. The General Assembly answered with clarity and continuing relevance: "The Scriptures may have their authority discredited not merely by a violation of their precepts, but also by any attempt on the part of ecclesiastical courts to bind the consciences of God's people on matters of doubtful interpretation."[23]

Women were finally ordained to all offices of the church, by 1956 in the Presbyterian Church in the U.S.A. and by 1965 in the PCUS. The new understanding of scripture embodied in those actions was made confessional in "A Brief Statement of Faith—Presbyterian Church (U.S.A.)," adopted in 1991. It explicitly affirms that the Spirit "calls women and men to all the ministries of the Church." A changed worldview was articulated in lines 29–32: "In sovereign love God created the world good and makes everyone equally in God's image, male and female, of every race and people, to live as one community."[24] With the new lens of the life and ministry of Christ, Presbyterians could finally see that God possessed the qualities of a mother as well as a father: "Loving us still, God makes us heirs with Christ of the covenant. Like a mother who will not forsake her nursing child, like a father who runs to welcome the prodigal home, God is faithful still."[25]

How Our Minds Have Changed

What does it take to overcome culture with the viewpoint of Christ? For a few, the change was dramatic and immediate. Paul got knocked to the ground by a blinding light. Christ taught Paul that the people he had been persecuting, because they didn't conform to his culture's laws, were the very people that God loved.

Peter had a vision. God showed him that the people his culture classified as unclean were clean in God's sight. It was a Gentile, someone his Jewish culture had taught him to shun, who brought him the good news of God's inclusive love.

For most of us, change comes slowly and in small increments. It took over two hundred years for a change in the dominant American worldview regarding the status of African Americans and the role of women. Wars were fought; laws were changed; and slowly, ever so slowly, people came to realize that we had created caricatures of people to justify our exclusion of them from society. We said African Americans were ignorant, vicious, and promiscuous to justify denying them education, subjecting them to inhumane conditions, and disrupting the possibility of normal family life. We said women were not rational and were unprepared for public life in order to deny them access to education and restrict their service to homemaking and child care. We justified these cultural prejudices in the name of God and on the basis of the Bible.

We have learned. We have changed our minds. We need to note carefully the factors that have made change possible. We gave up basing our view of slavery and the subordination of women on biblical descriptions of ancient Near Eastern culture that were then applied directly to our culture.

The Bible must *not* be read as a divine computer printout sent directly to us. Scripture is the record of a real God speaking to real people. We learn not only what God said but also what the people heard. They modified and manipulated the divine message to fit into their cultural setting, just as we do. We need to understand all texts in their historical and cultural context. When we make application to our life, we need to be aware of our own cultural conditioning. When we seek guidance, we need to look to the great themes of scripture rather than their ancient cultural applications.

How do we know what the great themes are? Look at Jesus. He continually defied the norms of his culture and interpreted the Old Testament law to accept and include those whom his culture rejected—Samaritans, women, tax collectors, lepers. The list goes on and on. We have been better able to see what God is saying in scripture when we have viewed all of it through the lens of Jesus' life and ministry.

The Influence of Contemporary Culture

We all understand and acknowledge that our culture obscured our seeing Christ's attitude toward slavery and the role of women. What are the areas in which our sight is blurred by our culture today? One possible area is homosexuality. Most Americans have been taught by our culture that all homosexual behavior is unnatural, perverse, and sinful. That is the usually unconscious assumption that most of us have.

Let us go back to where we began this essay, with Romans 1. We recognized that Romans 1:18–20 does not answer the theoretical, philosophical question of how God is known. Does Romans 1:24–27 answer the theoretical question of what homosexuality is? Does it intend to describe contemporary Christians who live in faithful, monogamous relations with someone of the same sex?

What is the practical point of Romans 1? All of us are sinners. None of us is more acceptable than others because of nature or culture or keeping the law. The point of Romans is that we are saved by grace that we receive only through faith.

We misuse scripture when we ask it theoretical questions that it was never intended to answer. Paul, in Romans 1:22 ff., is talking about a central problem in his culture, namely, idolatry—making graven images of people or birds or animals or reptiles. Then he appears to give an example of the worst kind of idolatry in his culture, where people worshiped false gods by having sex with prostitutes in the name of worship. To use Romans 1:26–27 as a proof text that in our culture all homosexual conduct is sinful misdirects us from the point of the passage—we who judge others are doing the very same sinful things (Rom. 1:32–2:1).

We should be sobered by how wrong we were for so long regarding African Americans and women. We live in a culture that similarly stereotypes homosexuals. By law and societal pressure, we prevent gay and lesbian people from having faithful, monogamous relationships, and then we accuse them of being inherently promiscuous. We bar them from exercising leadership in the church, and then we argue that they wouldn't make good role models. We use phrases popular in our culture, such as "the homosexual lifestyle," and then ignore the faithful lifestyles of ordinary, devout gay and lesbian Christian people.

Reading the Bible and reflecting on history makes me very uncomfortable these days. I have to ask myself if we are falling back on the earlier, repudiated practice of proof-texting. Every time we have excluded a class of people from full participation in the life of the church, we have later had to admit we were wrong. I wonder how we can exclude a whole class of people now in light of the life and ministry of Jesus.

When we understand the kind of knowledge we have in scripture and how it comes to us, we are blessed. God offers us salvation and bids us welcome cultural outcasts as neighbors. We receive that good news not by taking texts out of their ancient biblical context but by seeing all of scripture through the lens of Jesus Christ's accepting life and ministry.

NOTES

1. *Book of Confessions*, 6.007; hereafter *BC*.
2. *BC* 6.001.
3. See T. H. L. Parker, *Commentaries on the Epistle to the Romans*,

1532-1542 (Edinburgh: T. & T. Clark, 1986), where he compares the commentaries written by six Roman Catholics and five Reformers on three central passages, including Rom. 1:18–23.

4. *BC* 6.007.
5. Ibid., 6.006.
6. See Jack Rogers, *Reading the Bible and the Confessions: The Presbyterian Way* (Louisville, Ky.: Geneva Press, 1999), 11–12.
7. Jack B. Rogers and Donald K. McKim, *The Authority and Interpretation of the Bible: An Historical Approach* (San Francisco: Harper & Row, 1979), 23; hereafter AIB. Rev. ed. (1998) available from Wipf & Stock Publishers, 150 West Broadway, Eugene, OR 97401.
8. *BC* 6.007.
9. Ibid., 6.008.
10. Ibid.
11. Jack Rogers, *Claiming the Center: Churches and Conflicting Worldviews* (Louisville, Ky.: Westminster John Knox Press, 1995), 3.
12. Robert Ellis Thompson, *A History of the Presbyterian Churches in the United States*, The American Church History Series, 6 (New York: Christian Literature Co., 1895), 362–63.
13. John W. Christie and Dwight Dumond, *George Bourne and the Book and Slavery Irreconcilable*, Presbyterian Historical Society Series, 9 (Wilmington, Del.: Historical Society of Delaware, 1969), 61.
14. "Address of the General Assembly of the Presbyterian Church in the Confederate States of America to All the Churches of Jesus Christ Throughout the Earth," adopted unanimously at the Organization of the General Assembly in Augusta, Georgia, December 1861 (N.p.: Published by order of the Assembly, n.d.), 14.
15. Ibid., 11. For more on Thornwell and the Presbyterian defense of slavery, see Rogers, *Reading the Bible and the Confessions*, 73–77.
16. Robert L. Dabney, "Anti-Biblical Theories of Rights," *Presbyterian Quarterly* 2, no. 2 (July 1888): 217–19.
17. "Report of the Ad Interim Committee on a Biblical Study of the Position of Women in the Church" (*Minutes*, PCUS, 1956, p. 141).
18. "A Declaration of Faith (Presbyterian Church in the United States)," in *The Proposed Book of Confessions with Related Documents*, approved by the 116th General Assembly and recommended to the Presbyteries for their advice and consent (Atlanta: Presbyterian Church in the United States, 1976), chap. 2, 11.122–25.
19. Ibid., chap. 6, 11.65–67.

20. Extract from Minutes of the General Assembly, 1803–1811, 310, cited in Karen (Bear) Ride Scott, "Expanding the Horizons of Ministry: Women of the Cloth in the Presbyterian Church, U.S.A." (D.Min. diss., San Francisco Theological Seminary, 1990), 84.
21. Lois A. Boyd and R. Douglas Brackenridge, *Presbyterian Women in America: Two Centuries of a Quest for Status*, Contributions to the Study of Religion, no. 9, A Publication of the Presbyterian Historical Society (Westport, Conn.: Greenwood Press, 1983), 6.
22. Ronald W. Hogeland, "Charles Hodge: The Association of Gentlemen and Ornamental Womanhood, 1825–1855," *Journal of Presbyterian History* 53, no. 3 (fall 1975): 248.
23. *Minutes* of the General Assembly (1916) of the Presbyterian Church in the United States, 76, 80A; cited in Boyd and Brackenridge, *Presbyterian Women in America*, 211–12.
24. *BC* 10.4; 10.3, ll. 29–32.
25. *BC* 10.3, ll. 47–51.

Where Do You
Get That Living Water?

John 4:1–42

Sheila C. Gustafson

On this day, when the *Mission Yearbook for Prayer and Study* calls for a celebration of the gifts of women, it is fitting that our scripture should be the meeting of Jesus with the Samaritan woman at the well, because her character development represents a response to one of the most profound gifts of the Christian faith. It is also fitting that we should celebrate today (March 7, 1999) with the Presbyterian Church of Brazil as they move to ordain women as ministers for the first time in their history, for they reap, albeit belatedly, the harvest that was symbolically sown by that same Samaritan woman.

I warn you that the Gospel of John is complex and works on many levels. And, especially important for understanding this story, it often is not operating in real time. Here, what seems to be an episode from Jesus' life and ministry told by a contemporary narrator is, in actuality, a composition written decades later by the Gospel writer, who has included events that have happened since Jesus' death and resurrection and the concerns and realities of his own early Christian community.

To grasp the significance of this story, it is important to know that Jews and Samaritans despised each other. The split between the two groups was centuries old by Jesus' time, though they had both come out of the Mosaic tradition of Judaism. Like many denominational fights of our own experience, the Jerusalem Jews and the Samaritan Jews had divided over a theological issue—in their case, the proper location for the central worship of God. The Samaritans never bought into the David traditions that located the Temple in Jerusalem. In about 200 B.C.E., they had built their temple on Mount Gerizim north of Jerusalem, in Samaria. But in 128 B.C.E. it was destroyed by the Jerusalem Jews, who accused the Samaritans of false worship. Through the years, the perceived offenses of each side against the other built and built, until, when Jesus was conducting his ministry, it would have been difficult to find an example of a person more beneath the contempt of a religious Temple Jew than a Samaritan.

Although Luke's Gospel, probably written by and for Gentile readers, tells of Jesus using Samaritans as positive examples on a couple of occasions, Mark and Matthew were careful to indicate that Jesus, like any good Jew, stayed away from Samaria as he carried out his ministry. Matthew 10:5 and 6 says, in fact, "These twelve Jesus sent out with the following instructions: 'Go nowhere among the Gentiles, and enter no town of the Samaritans, but rather go to the lost sheep of the house of Israel.'"

But something remarkable happened among the followers of Jesus after the resurrection and their Pentecost experience. As, filled with the Holy Spirit and brimming over with the radical implications of Jesus' life and teaching, they shared the good news in Jerusalem, serious Jewish opposition grew in the city— and then persecution, personified by the man Saul who later experienced a conversion of his own and became known as Paul. To escape the danger, the new Christians decided to take their message out in ever-expanding circles from Jerusalem, and in due course, Philip arrived in Samaria—where, wonder of wonders, the Samaritans heard his testimony to Jesus Christ eagerly and were converted in droves. You can read the story in Acts 8.

By the time John wrote his Gospel, then, he was aware that there was a significant community of Samaritan Christians in existence. He realized that faith in Jesus Christ had been able to overcome a hatred between two peoples whose historic divisions were deep and bitter but who now, Jews and Samaritans alike—and Gentiles as well, for that matter—understood themselves to be one in Christ.

As John wrote, he communicated his community's experience. Nicodemus, the representative, upright, law-abiding Jew, had been offered by Jesus the new life of faith and had been closed to its possibilities. Now, in chapter 4, John sets up another encounter—this one in sharp contrast to the one with Nicodemus. That one had been in the dark; this one takes place when the sun is at its zenith—at noonday. That one had been with a perfect representative of establishment Judaism; this one is with as extreme an example of the disestablished human being as John could have imagined—a Samaritan, a woman, and one who had a "disorderly life," as one commentator put it.[1] Jesus enters into a serious theological discussion with each of these characters. The teacher of Israel never catches on to what Jesus is saying, or he refuses to catch on; but the Samaritan woman, after a few misunderstandings, gets it and not only gets it but realizes that good news of such magnitude has to be shared with others. She rushes off to tell her fellow Samaritans, who come to meet Jesus on the strength of her testimony and, on spending time with Jesus themselves, become true believers. The Samaritan woman thus becomes, according to the criteria of John's Gospel, a genuine evangelist and disciple.

This is a wonderful example of how the early Christians continued to experience the revelation of God through the risen Christ and incorporated their new insights and understandings into their accounts of the origins of their faith. All of the Gospel writers did that to some extent, but John's Gospel, because it is probably the last to be written, shows most clearly the ongoing activity of the Spirit with the church.

John's story is exquisitely drawn. Arriving at Jacob's well in Samaria at high noon, a tired and thirsty Jesus sat resting and hoping that someone would come along who had a bucket with which to draw water. Jacob had been an ancient enough religious figure to be venerated by the Samaritans as well as the Jews. Not surprisingly, since drawing water was women's work, the one who came along was a Samaritan woman.

Jesus asked for a drink of water to slake his physical thirst. The woman was shocked for several reasons—no Jewish man would initiate a conversation with a foreign woman; no Jew would drink from a Samaritan vessel; and no rabbi, which this turned out to be, would have a conversation in public with any woman. Yet Jesus had asked her to meet a simple need for him.

Jesus responded to her incredulity by, in essence, announcing a new state of things—although cryptically: "If you knew the gift of God, and who it is that is saying to you, 'Give me a drink,' you would have asked him, and he would have given you living water." In that moment, the reconciliation for which God's people waited and which they expected in the end times became real. The work of the resurrected Christ—the reconciliation of ancient enemies, the removal of distinctions of gender or race or other differences among God's people—had begun. And she, the woman of Samaria, was being offered in that moment, to meet *her* need, the benefits of the rule of God. But the metaphor of "living water" confused her at first.

How could this man give her water of any kind, not to mention spring water, when he didn't even have a bucket? Was he a wonder worker? And, since she was still caught up in the rivalry between their two peoples, was he implying that he, a Jew, was able to do greater things than her ancestor Jacob?

"Everyone who drinks of this water will be thirsty again," Jesus said, referring to physical thirst, "but those who drink of the water that I will give them will never be thirsty. The water that I will give will become in them a spring of water gushing up to eternal life." He was soon to demonstrate that he knew and understood the thirst of one who was spiritually dry.

Still uncertain what the man was getting at, the woman called his bluff, "Sir, give me this water, so that I may never be thirsty or have to keep coming here to draw water."

Then Jesus, from the woman's point of view, seemed to change the subject completely. "Go, call your husband, and come back," he said to her.

"I have no husband." A sensitive subject.

"You are right in saying, 'I have no husband'; for you have had five husbands, and the one you have now is not your husband."

Much has been made of the Samaritan woman's sexual history—but notice, there is no judgment here from Jesus, just a statement of fact; just another indication that he might really know her need for something transforming in her life. She has known estrangement—from her dominant society, from her immediate community, from God, probably even from herself.

The man's capacity to know everything about her and still be willing to engage her in conversation at last impressed the woman. He must be a prophet at least. Remarkably for her time and place, her gender, her station in life, the woman of Samaria grabbed the opportunity to ask a theological question. What about this issue that has divided the Jews and the Samaritans so bitterly for all this time? Where is it that we must worship God, on this mountain or in Jerusalem?

"Neither on this mountain nor in Jerusalem" was Jesus' response. The Spirit of God transcends all physical place—God's presence is available to all who worship in spirit and in truth—God, in fact, seeks out those who are ready to receive God's acceptance and love.

You mean, in the future, when the Messiah comes, God will do this.

I mean now, in the present, God is doing this. The Messiah (the Christ) is here, speaking with you.

Could it be true? But she had just experienced the results of exactly what Jesus was describing. The division between Jew and Samaritan had been breached, as well as that between male and female. The prophet had known all about her past and had offered her God's eternal life. He had even removed the distinctions of place and the limits of time. As they had talked, God had been present with them.

Even as Jesus' disciples arrived on the scene, dragging back with them all the limitations of the old evil age, the woman ran to share her good news with the people of the city. "Come and see," she said, using the discipleship language of John, "come and see a man who told me everything I have ever done! He cannot be the Messiah, *can he*?"

And they came, and they saw, and they believed for themselves; and they said, "This is truly the Savior of the world."

Nearly two thousand years ago, John the Evangelist told this story to help his church appreciate the new dispensation in which they lived. Christ is risen and is, with Christ's church, breaking down the divisions among people, removing the old prejudices and limitations, freeing people from the chains of their pasts. Jesus was able to make use of the gifts of a woman—a religiously and socially ostracized woman—to bring God's people to salvation.

Recently, in the Independent Presbyterian Church of Brazil, the way was made clear for women to be ordained as ministers. The good news is that the spirit of the risen Christ has broken down barriers and erased divisions among God's people. The bad news is that our world is mightily resistant to acknowledging that reality. We rejoice in this affirmation of the Spirit in Brazil and everywhere we see signs that the rule of God is breaking in. And we celebrate the gifts of women on this day in the calendar of the Presbyterian Church (U.S.A.). We also celebrate the gifts of men, and of children, and of people of color, and of people who are differently abled. Yet, even as we celebrate, we are aware of those whose talents and commitments are not officially welcomed and received in our churches, and we wonder: How long, O Lord, will it take for us to fully accept the gift made to your people so long ago?

In the Spirit of the risen Christ, all barriers are broken down—the barriers of race, of limiting theological difference, of gender, of sexual orientation, of status, of ability, of past estrangement, even of space and of time. In this moment, in this place, around this table, Christ is present and is offering to us the living water of eternal life. Christ is saying to *all* who would come:

Eat this bread, drink this cup; come to me and never be hungry.
Eat this bread, drink this cup; trust in me and you will not thirst.[2]

Amen.

NOTES

1. Gerard Sloyan, *John*, Interpretation: A Bible Commentary for Teaching and Preaching (Atlanta: John Knox Press, 1988), 54.
2. From *Music from Taizé, vol. II* (Taizé, France: Les Presses de Taizé, 1984).

Biblical Authority

Genesis 1:1–5; Colossians 2:6–11

Laird J. Stuart

We often talk in the church about authority of the Bible. We speak about biblical authority. We do this because we believe the Bible has a special authority for our life. Because of our faith in this authority, we read from the Bible every time we worship; we teach the Bible in our church school to our children; and every Sunday, we have some opportunity for adults to grow in their knowledge of the Bible.

Yet our current debate over ordination standards has made it clear many of us do not know just what we mean when we speak about the authority of the Bible. We are not sure how to describe it and how it works.

When we say something has authority, we mean it has authority for our lives. It has an influence over our lives. It can shape and change our lives. There are basically two ways in which authority works in our lives: either by command or by choice. There are authorities we simply have to obey. This is especially true for children, who basically have to obey every adult they meet. But even adults have some authorities they have to obey, such as the law. For the most part, however, for adults authority is something we confer on someone or something. We grant authority over our lives to someone or something.

The way this works with people is fairly clear, although the process can be intricate and mysterious. The way in which we allow people to have authority in our lives is like the way in which we let the Bible have authority.

Someone gains authority in our lives when we discover they tell the truth. When we meet someone who tells the truth, who is a reliable source of truth even if it inconveniences them or us, we begin to trust that person. The more we trust that person the more we rely on them. The more we rely on a person, the more we sense a kind of allegiance to them. If our trust in them grows sufficiently, we may even be willing to obey them in the sense that we might follow their advice or counsel, even if it contradicts what we want to do.

Of course, there are other factors involved when a person acquires authority in our lives. If, in addition to being a reliable and trustworthy source of truth, the person cares for us, so much the better. Furthermore, if the person is a reliable and trustworthy source of truth, cares for us, and has the capacity to help us, he or she will gain even more authority in our lives.

The Bible gains authority in our lives in the same way. It gains authority as we discover it is a source of truth, a reliable source of truth. We can also say it brings grace and goodness to us. We can also say it brings a power to our lives that helps us.

But it is the truth we find in the Bible, over and over again, that makes it increasingly reliable for us and that allows us to give it more and more authority for our lives. By this process, the Bible acquires the kind of authority by which it not only guides and inspires us but also disciplines us, changing us and challenging us to revise our beliefs and our behavior.

Essentially, the truth we find in the Bible is truth about God, truth about human nature, and truth about what happens when we are faithful to God and when we rebel against God.

We make a very special claim about the truth we find in the Bible. We claim it is revealed truth. It is truth that comes from God.

There are some passages in the Bible that have a truth you can recognize even if you do not believe in God. The Golden Rule, for instance, calling on us to treat other people as we would our-selves, is recognized as true by people who believe in God and by people who do not. The wisdom of so many of the stories told by Jesus, such as the story of the Good Samaritan, has a truth that is recognizable to people from within as well as outside the community of Christian faith.

Yet we believe the truth that can be found in Bible is not sim-ply the accumulated wisdom of humankind. It is truth that is given to the Bible by God. It is inspired truth. The Reformer John Calvin, who played such a prominent role in shaping the theology of Presbyterians, wrote, "Hence the scriptures obtain full authority among believers only when men regard them as having sprung from heaven."

The Bible contains truth God chose to speak and to reveal. The Bible is full of truth God wants to share with you and give to you.

Obviously, then, our belief in the authority of the Bible, a belief based on the truth we find in the Bible, is an act of faith, for we believe that truth comes from God.

Even people who agree that the Bible contains truth, truth that comes from God, do not always agree on just where that truth is found. It is fair to ask: Just where is the truth that comes from God to be found in the Bible?

Some people say the truth is essentially in the contents of the Bible.

One version of this view is that the Bible is God's revelation. Every word in it came from God just as it is written. Every word is true and right. The Bible is to be believed just as it is written.

Fortunately, there is a less extreme view of where the truth of God exists and can be found in the contents of the Bible. According to this view, the Bible is not God's revelation; the Bible is a record of God's revelation, an inspired record. Not every word in it is to be taken as truth. Yet God's truth is in the Bible, in the pages and in the passages.

According to this view, God's truth can be found in the con-cepts of the Bible, in how the Bible defines such concepts as

158   Laird J. Stuart

"peace," "justice," "forgiveness," and "church." According to this view, God's truth is found in the doctrines of the Bible, in doctrines such as the providence of God, the nature of Christ, the nature of sin, and the nature of free will. Another version of this belief is that God's truth is found in the great story of the Bible, in the whole unfolding drama of the Bible, and in the way in which it records how God works with us, seeks us, never controls us, but always receives us and works, often mysteriously, in this creation. One other version of the belief that God's truth is found in the contents of the Bible is the belief that truth is found in how the Bible, the Old and New Testaments, develops our understanding and image of Christ. It is in Christ, as Christ is presented in scripture, that we have the best source of God's truth for our lives.

Along with this belief that the truth of God is found in the contents of the Bible is another belief. It is not a contradictory or competing belief. It is the belief that God's truth is found in what the Bible does. What the Bible does is provide the stage for a living encounter between the people who read it and the God who is described in it.

There was a cartoon in the *New Yorker* magazine some years ago. It showed a large window in the side of a building. Over the window was a sign that read "Bible Bookstore." Inside the store, by the window, were stacks of Bibles. A sign was propped up against some of the Bibles. A woman on the sidewalk was looking through the window into the store; she had a puzzled look on her face. The sign declared, "Prepare to Meet the Author."

Another way in which truth comes to us in the Bible is through a living encounter with God as the Bible is read. When the great Lutheran minister Paul Scherer said that the Bible is a place of meeting, this is what he meant. Sometimes when you read the Bible, as inspiring as its contents can be, something even more inspiring and wonderful happens: God meets you. By the Holy Spirit, instead of reading about God and what God may have done with someone long ago, you sense the same God with you and beginning to do with you what God did with that someone else long ago. You might be reading a psalm written long ago by someone in some crisis, perhaps a crisis that sounds like your crisis, and suddenly, mysteriously and wonderfully, the sense of strength and care the psalmist gained from God begins to happen in your life. Or you might be reading about something that happened between someone and Christ. Again, as you read the story, you sense the person in the story is struggling with what you are struggling with, and then, as you read about how Christ touched and helped that person, in the same mysterious and wonderful manner, you sense Christ doing the same with you.

Sometimes when we are reading the Bible, by the work of God's Holy Spirit, we are no longer reading. We are relating to God, interacting with God, meeting and being blessed by God.

The Bible is authoritative for our lives because it has truth for our lives. Truth can be found in its contents and truth happens as we read it, happens in living encounters with God.

Even when we know the truth of God can be found in the Bible, however, another question arises: Just how can we discern in any given passage the truth from God for our lives?

Take, for example, the opening verses of the book of Genesis. These verses have been the stage for many debates about how to answer this question: How can we discern the truth from God for our lives?

Some people have suggested thinking of the Bible as a blueberry muffin. It is a big muffin. The blueberries are passages with God's truth for our lives. The dough is made up of passages that do not contain God's truth for our lives. The question is: How can you find the blueberries?

There are a number of guidelines or strategies that have been developed to help people find God's truth for their lives in the Bible. In 1982, our denomination approved a report on "Biblical Authority and Interpretation." It gave seven basic rules for interpreting scripture:

1. Recognize that Jesus Christ, the Redeemer, is the center of scripture. We are to keep Christ in the center of all discussions of the Bible and all struggles to find God's truth.

2. Let the focus be on "the plain sense of the text." This is a phrase from the Reformation. It means to focus on the text and listen to the text and avoid fanciful associations or allegories about the text.

3. Depend on the guidance of the Holy Spirit. The Holy Spirit is the necessary guide for us to find God's truth. Out of love, God gives us God's own Spirit to guide us to God's truth.

4. Be guided by the "rule of faith," that is, the teaching of the church. In your personal Bible study or in some group Bible study, you do not need to find out everything the church has taught over the years about a certain passage, but the basic creeds and doctrines of the church will give some background and breadth to your own discernment.

5. Let all interpretation be guided by the "rule of love." As passages are studied and sometimes debated, we are to work at loving God and loving one another in the process. One of the basic barriers to God's inspiration in our lives is our own pride, our pride in what we know, our pride in what we believe. A little more love for God and a little more love for one another would help immensely some of our interpretative efforts and debates.

6. Respect the need for "earnest study." Sometimes God can speak to us directly and quickly through scripture. But as a general rule, our confidence that we have found God's truth will be enhanced if we are willing to study a text and other views of a text, even after we may think we have come to know God's truth for us in it.

7. Seek to interpret a particular passage of the Bible in light of the whole Bible. It is always dangerous to assume that one passage, much less one verse, contains all the wisdom and inspiration God has to give us on some matter or subject.[1]

It is tempting, after hearing these seven steps, to think it all sounds like too much work. You may be wondering right now how on earth you can be expected to remember all that.

It may also be tempting to be offended that there is no mention here of human knowledge, such as the knowledge of science or of experience, and when we learn by experience.

These guidelines for interpretation are not meant to rule out human knowledge or the insights from our own experiences. Such knowledge and insights belong in the process of interpretation and are to be included in this process.

First, it should be said there are times when God speaks right to us, with a freshness and an immediacy that seem to deny the need for study. There certainly are times when God senses a hungering and desperate spirit opening these pages, and God, out of grace and love, speaks directly in the words that are read and meets directly with the person reading. You can open these pages sometimes and God's truth for your life is right there.

But it is also true that, very often, discerning God's truth takes time and takes effort. Now, you will spend time and effort in other enterprises. If you get a new Palm Pilot, you will spend God only knows how long trying to figure out how it works. You would do the same with some new software for your computer. You may work hard on a garden or on your golf game, your tennis game, or your bridge game. You will work hard on a relationship. You will work hard raising children. Sometimes you have to work like that with this Bible, to get to know it, to get to know how it works, to get to know how God speaks and acts through it.

The work is worth it. The result is worth it. Surely the benefits and blessings of having God's truth dawn on and warm your life are worth some seeking and searching!

Going back to the opening verses of Genesis, if you work at interpreting these verses, you will discover different views of God's truth for your life. There is the view some have suggested that the verses prove God loves baseball. After all, according to this view, the first four words in the Bible are, "In the big inning . . ." A more reverent view takes the position that these verses describe how creation happened and form a reliable record of the process of creation. Most people, however, have come to another view: it is the view that the truth from God for our lives is that God created. These verses are not about the "how" of creation. The science of evolution has taught us that.

These verses tell us "why" creation happened. Creation happened because God chose to create, because God willed to create.

Now, if you take this truth from the opening pages of Genesis, this truth that God creates, and track it through the Bible, you discover that God never stopped creating. God keeps on creating. God keeps working in God's world, and God keeps working with people. Then it can occur to you that the God who created and keeps on creating could be creating in your life, working in your life, rebuilding and repairing and renewing your life. So a truth from God revealed in the opening pages of Genesis becomes a source of inspiration and new life for you right now.

You can discern God's truth for your life. It may take some work, but you can do it.

There is one final word that must be added to any consideration of the authority of the Bible: it is that the authority of the Bible is not the final or supreme authority for our lives. The supreme authority for our faith and life is Christ.

This is what Paul was affirming in the letter to the Colossians. The supreme authority for our faith and life is in Christ. He is our surest defense against what Paul refers to as "empty deceit" and misleading "human tradition." He is "the head of every ruler and authority." The Bible has its own unique authority and will help us find and receive God's truth. But Christ is the surest help. We are to live our lives with Christ; we are to be "rooted and built up in him."

NOTE

1. *Biblical Authority and Interpretation*, bound together with *Presbyterian Understanding and Use of the Holy Scripture*, under the latter title. Published by the Presbyterian Church (U.S.A.). Available from Presbyterian Distribution Service, #OGA-92-003.

PART 5

Bound Together
in Christ's Name

Bound Together in Christ's Name

A Reformed Perspective on the Ecumenical Movement

Jane Dempsey Douglass

The ecumenical movement has gifted the twentieth-century churches around the globe with unprecedented opportunities to know and support one another, to bridge centuries-old divisions in a search for Christian unity and begin the healing of old wounds, and to bring fresh witness to the gospel both in churches and in the economic and social life of the world beyond the church. The Holy Spirit has been enlivening the churches and renewing them, helping them grasp the ways in which they are bound together in Christ's name.

Today, as Christians travel the world, they find a rich but sometimes bewildering diversity of churches identifying themselves as Christian, with many styles of liturgy, many forms of government and congregational life, and many ways of understanding the Bible. Think of a Pentecostal storefront church in any large American city, of a Scottish Presbyterian church much like some of our own, of St. Peter's Church in Rome, or a simple Catholic base community in Latin America, or an Orthodox church in the Middle East with its many icons, or an African independent congregation marching through the streets to plant its flag on an open space and worship outdoors. How can we recognize the church, the body of Christ, to which we are bound in Christ's name, to which we have obligations of unity in love? Do we recognize only those churches in which we immediately feel comfortable because they are like our own?

Our teacher John Calvin followed Martin Luther in identifying the distinguishing marks of the church as the preaching of the Word of God and the observance of the sacraments. For us, then, the challenge of the ecumenical movement must be to enter into a persistent, loving, patient, and honest engagement with all those who preach the gospel of Jesus Christ and administer the sacraments, seeking visible unity. We are not at liberty to select only those partners with whom we are comfortable and with whom we find greatest agreement. Rather, we are called to ecumenical engagement with all those companions on our pilgrimage whom God has called to accompany us. We cannot know precisely what form and shape our life together may finally take, since we believe the Holy Spirit is continually at work among us, making all things new. We undertake this engagement in search of unity in response to Christ's prayer for unity, in obedience to the call of the Spirit, repentant for our wounding the body of Christ by our unfaithfulness and by our disrespect for our sisters and brothers in Christ, believing that our witness will be made stronger. We are hopeful that before the *eschaton* we shall come to the day when we can sit together at the table spread by our common Lord, Jesus Christ. In the meantime, we are offered the precious gift of stimulating companions on our way who help our faith and our hearts and our minds to grow to meet new challenges.

In this essay I first identify the people whom I am calling Reformed, in order to remind us of our own family's diversity in unity, and sketch a classical Reformed vision of the unity of the church. Second, I describe briefly the Reformed relation to the modern ecumenical movement. Third, I suggest what local congregations can do to grasp more profoundly that we are all bound together in Christ.

The Reformed Family and Its Vision of the Church

The Reformed family is not a single church but rather a family of Reformed churches, one of which is the Presbyterian

Church (U.S.A.). These churches, some called Presbyterian, some called Reformed, and some called Congregational, are historically and theologically related to the sixteenth-century Genevan Reformation, whose principal teacher was the French theologian John Calvin. Two stem from pre-Reformation reforming movements: the Waldensians and the Czech Brethren. Calvin's teaching and the reforms in Geneva attracted enormous numbers of refugees and students from all over Europe, creating a very international community. As the refugees and students returned to their homelands, the Calvinist vision spread, and an international network of church leaders developed. Calvin was in conversation with the Swiss theologians who succeeded Huldrych Zwingli, and their consensus grew. The family of Protestant churches in the Swiss cantons and those stemming from Geneva soon came generally to be called Reformed, in distinction from the Lutheran churches. From its origins, then, the Calvinist or Reformed movement was international and culturally diverse.

Reformed churches in their different contexts went their own ways until the nineteenth century, when they began to meet one another on mission fields around the world. They felt the need in 1875 to create an alliance of churches in the Reformed family, the first and still the largest of the organized Protestant "Christian world communions." The overarching theme of the early years seems to be a search for Christian unity and for social justice, a search set in the context of passion for Christian witness and the worldwide mission of the church. The alliance urged its members not to perpetuate the confessional divisions of the West on the mission field; the newly planted churches should be rooted in the local culture and allowed to become independent as soon as possible and to join the alliance as independent churches. The alliance was self-conscious about its "catholicity" as well as its cultural diversity.[1]

Today, nearly three-fourths of the 217 member churches of the World Alliance of Reformed Churches are located in the countries of the south: Asia, Africa, and Latin America. In several countries of the north and the south, church leaders have heeded the urgings of the early alliance leaders and formed united churches, many of which are members of the World Alliance. Some of these, such as the Church of South India, brought together Reformed churches with churches of traditions that hold to the necessity of the historic episcopate. The alliance therefore has a challenging ecumenical component within its own structure.

Unity in diversity is characteristic of the Reformed family. For a classic statement of the Reformed vision of the church, we can turn to the Second Helvetic Confession of 1566,[2] widely recognized as authoritative in the Reformed family. In teaching about the Trinity and Christology, the creeds and decrees of the first four ecumenical synods of the ancient church are affirmed, along with the Athanasian Creed, as agreeing with scripture, the authority for faith (chap. 11, cf. chap. 2). In chapter 17, "Of the Catholic and Holy Church of God, and of the One Only Head of the Church," we hear repeatedly the insistence that there is only one church, that it has always existed and always will as an assembly of the faithful, the communion of saints:

And since there is always but one God, and there is one mediator between God and men [human beings], Jesus the Messiah, and one Shepherd of the whole flock, one Head of this body, and, to conclude, one Spirit, one salvation, one faith, one Testament or covenant, it necessarily follows that there is only one Church. . . . We, therefore, call this Church catholic because it is universal, scattered through all parts of the world, and extended unto all times, and is not limited to any times or places.

Believers "joined together with all the members of Christ by an unfeigned love . . . show that they are Christ's disciples by persevering in the bond of peace and holy unity" (chap. 17). There is "no certain salvation outside Christ," so believers should not be separated from the true church of Christ. Nevertheless, there is a recognition that circumstances, especially of repression, may make it impossible for all to participate in the sacraments. There also is a recognition that "God had some friends in the world outside the commonwealth of Israel." Though the church may at times seem to be extinct, and though there are persons in the visible church who are not true members of the church, we must be careful not to make too hasty judgments about those whom the Lord wishes to have excluded:

> [W]e diligently teach that care is to be taken wherein the truth and unity of the Church chiefly lies, lest we rashly provoke and foster schisms in the church. Unity consists not in outward rites and ceremonies, but rather in the truth and unity of the catholic faith. The catholic faith is not given to us by human laws, but by Holy Scriptures, of which the Apostles' Creed is a compendium. And, therefore, we read in the ancient writers that there was a manifold diversity of rites, but that they were free, and no one ever thought that the unity of the Church was thereby dissolved. So we teach that the true harmony of the Church consists in doctrines and in the true and harmonious preaching of the Gospel of Christ, and in rites that have been expressly delivered by the Lord [that is, baptism and the Lord's Supper]. (Chap. 17)

Once again, we hear the theme of the unity of the church in the gospel despite diversity.

Reformed Relation to the Ecumenical Movement

Reformed Christians, both pastors and lay people, were very active in the early ecumenical organizations of the late nineteenth and early twentieth centuries. These were largely voluntary movements made up of individual participants from many denominations, rather than of official church bodies—movements such as the Evangelical Alliance, the Student Volunteer Movement (for missions), and the World Student Christian Federation. Leaders of the World Alliance of Reformed Churches also were heavily engaged in the organizational activities leading up to the first meeting of the World Council of Churches (WCC) in 1948, which brought together a wide variety of Protestant as well as Orthodox churches. The first general secretary, Willem Visser 't Hooft, as well as many early leaders of the WCC, such as Hendrik Kraemer and Madeleine Barot, were Reformed. Commitment of Reformed churches to the WCC continues to be strong.

The attitude of the Alliance was clearly stated at the Princeton General Council of 1954: "We believe that the deep stirring among the churches and Christian groups to surmount the barriers and to express the unity of the community of believers in accordance with the mind and will of Jesus Christ, the Head of the Church . . . is of God, not men, a sign of the Holy Spirit."[3] This council also showed its intention that the World Alliance should expect to learn from others in ways that would allow mutual correction:

> The task of the Alliance is steadily to exhort the Reformed churches to have recourse to the Holy Scriptures; and then, if a renewed study of the Scriptures, pursued in common with brethren [and sisters] from other confessions, should disclose aspects of truth not yet apprehended, to be ready to accept them. If, on the other hand, the Reformed churches should become persuaded, through such a study of the Holy Scriptures, of an error in their own doctrinal positions, they should be ready likewise to acknowledge and abandon it.[4]

Again, at the General Council at Ottawa in 1982, the World Alliance reaffirmed its commitment:

> Faced by a plurality of churches throughout the world, we have a choice between claiming to be the one true church to which all others ought eventually to come and, on the other hand, seeking the fullness of Christ's Church by entering into dialogue and fellowship with those other churches which share with us the Gospel. As we may not claim a monopoly of the Gospel, there is for us no alternative to involvement in the ecumenical movement.[5]

Since the formation of the World Council of Churches, the Alliance has cooperated closely with the WCC. The Alliance has nonetheless seen a need to continue its work to gather together the Reformed family, to bring the witness of its theological tradition to the ecumenical movement, to represent the Reformed family in international ecumenical dialogue, to work for human rights and religious freedom, to be the advocate of Reformed churches under pressure in daunting situations, and to facilitate mutual assistance among the members of the Reformed family.

Beginning in the 1960s, the Roman Catholic Church stimulated a movement of bilateral dialogues among world communions. The goal is deeper mutual understanding and positive steps toward clearer expression of Christian unity. One remarkable accomplishment is that the Catholic Church and the Lutheran World Federation are in the final stage of completing a joint statement on justification by faith that would permit each to drop certain historical condemnations of the other. The World Alliance of Reformed Churches has been engaged in bilateral dialogues with all the Protestant world communions; dialogue with the Catholic and the Orthodox churches is ongoing. Recently, discussions were undertaken with Pentecostal leaders, though they have no organized world body.

Increasingly, these conversations will be multilateral, since what we say to one partner affects our relationship to other partners. There is a movement coming out of the WCC to launch in 2000 a forum of the various world Christian communions that would be broader than the WCC, in the hope of preparing the way for a truly ecumenical council. Such a forum would hope to include such major groups of Christians as those Pentecostal and "evangelical" churches that are not now members of the WCC, as well as the Roman Catholic Church, which participates in many WCC programs but is not a member.

So far, we have been focusing on ecumenical work at the world level. At the regional level, some Reformed churches have been able to establish concrete new relationships. In Europe since 1973, Lutheran and Reformed churches have enjoyed the experience of full communion and mutual recognition of ministries through the Leuenberg Agreement. This agreement now has been broadened and is being recognized elsewhere, for example, in Argentina. In North America, decades of dialogue intended to establish a similar relationship of full communion between the Reformed and Lutheran churches began in the 1960s. Finally, in 1998, we were able to celebrate the beginning of a relationship of full communion among the Evangelical Lutheran Church in America, the Reformed Church in America, the United Church of Christ, and the Presbyterian Church (U.S.A.).

Our own Presbyterian Church, led by Stated Clerk Eugene Carson Blake, along with the Episcopal Church in the United States, initiated in 1961 the bold proposal of a Consultation on Church Union (COCU), with the intention to bring about a union of the two churches. The number of churches participating grew to nine. Since the goal of organic union has seemed to be impossible to attain, the plan now is to create a covenant communion (Churches United in Christ) that will permit mutual recognition of sacraments and of ministries, witnessing together to common faith, and acting together in service. Because three of the churches are historically African American, in this context we have a special opportunity to confront and deal with the role of racism in dividing the church. The process of ratification of the covenant should be completed by 2002.

What Can Presbyterian Congregations Do?

1. Increasingly in ecumenical circles, there is a move toward thinking about unity in terms of fellowship or communion in the gospel within which differences are nonetheless recognized. This is very congenial to the Reformed spirit. We can foster this spirit as we approach other Christian churches but also when we see lines of division hardening among our people. We must remember that today most of our congregations are receiving many new members from other denominations, people whose religious backgrounds we may not understand and who may not be familiar with the Reformed tradition. There is ecumenical education to be done within our congregations.

2. The search for a deeper grasp of the gospel must go hand in hand with the search for unity as part of the renewal of the

church that the Holy Spirit is bringing about. It is paradoxical that at the same time that we are opening ourselves to understand more sympathetically differences around traditional, church-dividing issues such as the nature of the sacraments, we also through more profound commitment to justice, are recognizing that issues dealing with race and gender also are church-dividing. These issues in some cases have led to splinter movements, creating new denominations, or have hindered ecumenical rapprochement among denominations; in other cases they have created dissension and discord within denominations. Differences of conviction within denominations may be greater than differences across denominational lines.

For example, in the struggle against apartheid, the World Alliance of Reformed Churches declared in 1982 that the theological justification of apartheid is not merely an error but heresy, a deformation of the heart of Christian faith. Probably all Christian churches today would agree, but for some, the struggle to accept this has been very difficult and divisive. The ordination of women, too, remains a church-dividing issue. PC(USA)'s "A Brief Statement of Faith" makes clear that for us, recognition of God's call of women to all offices of the church is a confessional matter, a matter of faith related to the doctrine of the church, not simply a matter of polity (church rules or government). We feel compelled to witness to this conviction even though it does, in fact, create an obstacle to closer unity with some other churches, and it continues to create some debate within our own church. For many Christians, the issue of recognizing full rights of church membership, including eligibility for ordination, for gay and lesbian people professing Christian faith has become a similar matter of faith. All these issues remind us that it is God who calls people into faith and into the church; we must receive those called by God with gratitude as companions on our journey of faith, where each has something to give and something to receive.

The call to Christian unity must never become a pretext for avoiding the hard questions that the Spirit is raising among us as part of the renewal of the church. Reformed people believe that the church reformed according to the Word of God is always in need of reformation. But the call to Christian unity can become a fruitful context in which Christians of many traditions can deal with hard questions together, since they concern us all.

3. We can reach out to other congregations to make ecumenical commitments concrete at the grass roots. We can make contact with local churches of those Reformed bodies with which the Presbyterian Church (U.S.A.) is discussing possible steps toward merger: the Cumberland Presbyterian Church and the Korean Presbyterian Church in America. We also can contact local congregations of Reformed groups that have chosen not to participate ecumenically. Despite our "catholic" theology, Reformed people often have tried to solve their disagreements through division and splintering. We have a responsibility to help heal the schisms and overcome historic divisions within our own family.

We can reach out to congregations of our partner churches in COCU and to Lutheran congregations, devising ways to make national-level agreements vital in our local context. We can also reach out to the churches with which we are least familiar.

Local ecumenism is flourishing, demonstrating the life and vitality that can come from working together in response to God's call to justice. Local councils of churches often have outreach ministries to serve the poor and marginalized and to work for justice. Working with other Christians to find local solutions to problems of violence, homelessness, hunger, economic injustice, and environmental pollution can be a transforming experience. Ecumenical study groups also can be stimulating and energizing.

In another sense, the ecumenical aspects of our Christian faith must be regularly made visible in all local church life. Every baptism, for example, is an opportunity to help the congregation grasp that the one being baptized is entering the church universal. I once visited an international and interdenominational congregation in Sweden where the world community was vividly apparent in the diversity of dress and accent. On that Sunday a child was baptized. Afterward, the grandfather of the child declared how delighted he was to realize that his grandchild had been baptized into a community that includes Christians in all the world, of many Christian traditions. But then he reflected soberly, "But of course that is true of all baptisms! Why did I never realize this before?" Why indeed? How can we help church members gain a broader sense of Christian identity rooted in the one holy catholic church, where there is one Lord, one faith, one baptism? Surely personal contact with Christians of other lands and of other communions is essential and should be fostered with care and imagination. One way in which these ties are being cultivated is through presbytery partnerships with overseas churches. A warning, however: any mission projects overseas must be planned and carried out in a manner fully respectful of the church already at work in that place, with careful consultation and genuine partnership. Americans need to be aware that the need to be always in control is a spiritual problem.

The Ecumenical Church

In conclusion, we turn once more to the nature of the ecumenical movement. It is a response to the renewing movement of the Holy Spirit among us. Though it is not an organization, it creates activities and organizations. Christians sense that the Spirit is moving us toward one another to heal old schisms and renew our life. By its nature, this renewing force wells up in our churches, disrupting our familiar patterns of life, raising new questions. But it also arises in other surprising places, giving poor and marginalized people in our churches and outside them the courage to cry out for justice. The very creation itself seems now to be crying out for justice.

Not all cries in the church or the world today are from the urging of the Holy Spirit. We must try together, with prayer and the guidance of the scriptures, to discover what is of God. The scriptures tell us that the reign of Christ is a reign of unity, of peace and love, but also of justice, of wholeness for the entire restored creation. In contrast, the churches are divided within, even more than along, denominational lines as they struggle to address the realities of global economic injustice, injustice for women, injustice for racial and ethnic minority groups, injustice for gay and lesbian people, global warming and other environmental damage, and refugee movements. American Christians need to learn from their sisters and brothers from the Southern Hemisphere, in Asia, Africa, and Latin America, how they experience these problems in their own lives; if Americans are truly able to hear, they will never look at the world in the same way again. Some Christians from the South, for example, despairing of the new global economy where the rich get richer and the poor get poorer, are arguing that economic justice is such a fundamental teaching of Christian faith that acceptance of economic injustice as inevitable is a rejection of Christian faith. The ecumenical movement is helping us understand that Christians must address such questions together, drawing on the different experiences of us all.

The ecumenical institutions we have created will have to be continually renovated as our vision grows and our churches change. The WCC is now engaged in such revision, and others will do so. It seems clear that many of our structures are neither largely nor broadly enough conceived for the task to be done, though they may have grown too big in size and cost.[6] They must be hospitable to the whole family of God, enabling the family members in their diversity to address with integrity the whole range of issues that divide us—issues of Christology and ecclesiology; issues of culture, race, and gender; issues of social justice and the integrity of creation. Our reconciliation is integrally related to our witness to the world.

Structures themselves, however, do not reconcile. Faithful Christians must design and inhabit those structures. While not losing the momentum of progress already made among churches active in the ecumenical movement, we must reach out to include churches now on the margins. We need to identify and respect the vital voluntary reforming movements outside formal structures as well, asking what word of God they may have for the churches. It was the energy of movements such as these that launched the modern ecumenical movement a century ago.

Yet we must not lose our focus on the role of the churches themselves in expressing the mutual interdependence of the members of the body of Christ. All churches are constrained by the gospel to work for the full mutual recognition that will permit us to sit together at the table of our Lord, demonstrating to the world that we are bound together in Christ. Though this work is often slow and difficult, by the grace of God there is also great joy and enrichment in coming to know our sisters and brothers in Christ, in accompanying them and being accompanied by them as we struggle to make the reign of God more visible.

NOTES

1. See Marcel Pradervand, *A Century of Service: A History of the World Alliance of Reformed Churches, 1875–1975* (Grand Rapids: Wm. B. Eerdmans Publishing Co., 1975), chaps. 1–5.
2. Quotations from the Second Helvetic Confession are taken from *Reformed Confessions of the 16th Century*, ed. Arthur C. Cochrane (Philadelphia: Westminster Press, 1966). The confession can also be found in the PC(USA) *Book of Confessions*.
3. Lukas Vischer, "The Ecumenical Commitment of the World Alliance of Reformed Churches," *Reformed World* 38 (1985): 262.
4. Ibid., 274.
5. Ibid., 267.
6. This is a common theme in current writing about the ecumenical movement. See, for example, Konrad Raiser, *Ecumenism in Transition: A Paradigm Shift in the Ecumenical Movement?* (Geneva: WCC Publications, 1991); H. S. Wilson and Nyambura J. Njoroge, eds., *New Wine: The Challenge of the Emerging Ecclesiologies to Church Renewal* (Geneva: World Alliance of Reformed Churches, 1994); Teresa Berger, "The Church in the World: Ecumenism: Postconfessional? Consciously Contextual?" *Theology Today* 53 (1996): 213–19; S. Mark Heim, "The Next Ecumenical Movement," *Christian Century*, August 14–26, 1996, 780–83; Lewis S. Mudge, *The Sense of a People: Toward a Church for the Human Future* (Philadelphia: Trinity Press International, 1992); Lewis S. Mudge, *Renewing the Ecumenical Vision*, Theology and Worship Occasional Paper no. 7 (Louisville, Ky.: Presbyterian Church (U.S.A.), n.d.).

"Through Times of
Challenge, Controversy, and Hope"

Deborah F. Mullen

W hen the modern ecumenical movement was launched in the early 1950s in America, it solidified an organizational presence through which mainline Protestant churches and the historic black churches could act together on public issues such as racial prejudice and segregation.[1] The ecumenical movement of the late 1950s and the 1960s exercised its influence widely in the affairs of the nation, signifying the powerful role that Protestant churches played in American life. It was not until the Civil Rights movement championed the cause of racial justice, however, that the National Council of Churches (NCC) and its member churches became an activist force in America's black freedom movement. Presbyterians were among the first of the mainstream Protestant churches to become involved in campaigns of "direct action" to dramatize the plight of disenfranchised African American citizens who were, more important, sisters and brothers in the body of Christ.[2]

As part of an ongoing project to learn more about how we "reunited" Presbyterians have worked together ecclesiastically and ecumenically on issues of racial justice at various time during our history, I have selected a period that spans thirty years in the life of the Northern stream of the denomination, from the late 1940s to the mid-1970s, to illustrate two things: (1) the impact of our church's public witness on wider society and (2) the enduring legacy of our church's commitment, however problematic and fraught with internal conflicts, to the pursuit of racial justice and the realization of Christian unity.   Although the struggle for justice continues and the many tensions surrounding Christian unity have yet to be resolved, our history as a denomination reveals that as black and white Presbyterians, we are sisters and brothers who are bound together in Christ's name "through times of controversy, challenge, and hope!"

New Occasions Teach New Duties

Americans share a national identity shaped by a myriad of social factors, including race. Cornel West, the popular African American philosopher, has written extensively on the race question and how skin color, particularly "whiteness" and "blackness," have been viewed and have functioned in American life. In the best-seller *Race Matters,* however, West explodes the myth that race is *all* that matters. Writing after the 1992 "upheaval" in Los Angeles, West exposes racism and white superiority as twin threats to the democratic social order and the cultural ideals of freedom and equality.[3] West writes:

> To engage in a serious discussion of race in America, we must not begin with the problems of black people but with the flaws of American society—flaws rooted in historic inequalities and longstanding cultural stereotypes. How we set up the terms for discussing racial issues shapes our perception and response to these issues. As long as black people are viewed as a "them," the burden falls on blacks to do all the "cultural" and "moral" work necessary for healthy race relations. The implication is that only certain Americans can define what it means to be American—and the rest must simply "fit in."[4]

Try as we may, we have failed as a nation to address the deep fissure between the races and to redress the underlying social, political, and economic causes and systems that have supported racial injustice for more than four hundred years. Evidently,

180 Deborah F. Mullen

W. E. B. DuBois was correct in his assessment of America's obsession with the "color line" at the end of the nineteenth century.[5] DuBois's social analysis *The Souls of Black Folk*, first published in 1903, is no less penetrating and prophetic nearly one hundred years later, at the dawning of the twenty-first century.

Protestant churches in the United States have long reflected many of the same customs, values, and prejudices as those found in dominant society. The uneasy and often distrustful relationship between American Christians of African and European descent reveals our inability as a nation and as a people of faith to deal with racial difference as something more than just another social problem. Given our history as a racially divided nation, whites and blacks remain ambivalent over whether racial reconciliation is a goal to be hoped for now or in the foreseeable future.

Black Christians come to their ambivalence from several angles. Mainline churches have been slow to attack the racial prejudice of their members, who were often in denial about their own complicity in the perpetuation of racism but who were unquestionably the beneficiaries of white privilege in the church and society. Black members in denominations such as the Presbyterian Church (U.S.A.) have felt betrayed by a lack of willingness or moral courage on the part of their white sisters and brothers to renounce white racism as sin and exorcise it from the body of Christ. Members of historically black churches are rightfully critical of the ways in which racism has deformed the body of Christ, held the gospel captive, and served to distort the image of the African American Christian tradition by characterizing it as somehow an inferior Christianity to that practiced by white Christians.

White Christians speak of their ambivalence in very different terms, according to Nibs Stroupe, pastor of Oakhurst Presbyterian Church outside Atlanta, Georgia. Stroupe and Inez Fleming, an African American member of the congregation, are coauthors of an important book on their experience as a multiracial fellowship of Christians in the South. He writes that those of us called white are tired of race. Most of us believe that we have done enough to make the idea of equality a reality in this society. We made great shifts during the civil rights movement, and we continue to try to see all people as our equals. Yet, we continue to hear from people of darker color, especially African-American people, that racism is strong and even growing. This is harsh news for us. It is a source of frustration and despair for white people.[6]

Tired or not, racism, like all sin, is devastating in its ability to alienate us from one another and from our God; it stands in the way of *shalom*. Even the most sincere of those whose mission and ministry are devoted to racial reconciliation become overwhelmed and discouraged from time to time in the struggle to eradicate racism from church and society. The sin of racism is debilitating and ultimately deforming but can be transformed through repentance. The manifestation of a changed spirit and new creation is God's gift in the conversion process. The church of Jesus Christ is called to repent, to be converted, and to become that new creation in the world! That is the vision we Presbyterians are called to embrace for our own renewal as a theologically diverse, multiracial, and multicultural community of faith, always being reformed according to God's purpose, "so that the world may believe" (John 17:21).

That All May Freely Serve

In many ways it has fallen to voluntary associations, such as religious organizations (e.g., churches, synagogues, mosques, meetinghouses), to contend with society over its shoddy treatment of African Americans, to ameliorate the harsh realities of being looked on as "black outsiders" and second-class citizens, and to defend the highest principles of democracy. In March 1946, the Federal Council of Churches, offspring of the Social Gospel movement and precursor of the National Council of Churches, adopted "a non-segregated church and a non-segregated society"[7] as its official policy and goal for its member churches. The Presbyterian Church U.S.A. immediately followed suit.

For nearly forty years (1946–1983), many Presbyterians in both North and South became strategically engaged in ministries of public witness and social action as a theological response to racial injustice and as a political tool to advance the highest goals of the democratic social order: freedom and equality. Early in the 1950s, efforts to promote racial integration by these Presbyterians and the National Council of Churches collided head-on with national policy, drawing considerable backlash from within and outside the churches. As momentum gathered to overturn "separate but equal"—the law upholding racial segregation since the 1896 U.S. Supreme Court decision in *Plessy v. Ferguson*—many white Presbyterian clergy and denominational leaders became "sympathetic allies" with African American church people in their fight for freedom.[8] Ironically, what had started out in the minds of many as "the agitation for Negro rights in America" was becoming a broad-based interracial, ecumenical, and interfaith campaign for the civil and human rights of all Americans.[9]

Throughout American history religious persons, leaders and laity, have exercised their faith convictions in the public realm for the common good in a manner that has come to be known as "public religion."[10] Dr. John Witherspoon, president of the College of New Jersey and signer of the Declaration of Independence is an example. More recently, one whose public witness on racial justice issues and whose leadership in the ecumenical movement pushed Presbyterians to civic prominence in the 1960s was Stated Clerk Eugene Carson Blake.

Gene Blake served for more than a decade as stated clerk of the Presbyterian Church in the United States of America (after the merger of 1958, the United Presbyterian Church in the U.S.A. [UPCUSA]). He is probably best known as the visionary whose December 4, 1960, sermon was the seed that led to the formation of the Consultation on Church Union (COCU) in 1962. Several years later, as general secretary of the World Council of Churches (1966–1972), Blake's passion for racial justice figured decisively in the WCC's unprecedented action to adopt and fund the *Programme to Combat Racism* (PCR) in 1969. PCR embodied the ecumenical movement's commitment to eradicate racism as a necessary step in fulfilling the church's calling to unity and justice as the manifestation of God's reign in the world.[11]

Earlier in life, in 1940, Pastor Gene Blake refused to sign a racially restrictive neighborhood covenant when he moved his family from Albany, New York, to the then-influential Pasadena Presbyterian Church (PPC). After he had been at PPC for a number of years, Blake was enlisted by the Interracial Council of the Pasadena Council of Social Agencies to lend his support and leadership to their mission "to secure for minorities the full rights and privileges of citizens of the community" and "to get members of minority groups to assume responsibility of citizenship within the community." Eugene Carson Blake had come a long way since his beginnings in racially segregated St. Louis, where he first experienced the "wrongness of social prejudice."[12]

He was not afraid to take the necessary steps toward a racially inclusive church, even if it meant having to fire those who refused to comply. In his third year as stated clerk, the same year that the U.S. Supreme Court rendered its historic decision in *Brown v. Board of Education* (1954), Blake issued the first executive order mandating that the Office of the General Assembly be integrated.[13] Nevertheless, according to one African American director of a major program, Blake never darkened his door the whole time they worked together in the same building during the early 1960s. Yet, in the decade that he served as president of the National Council of Churches, chairman of its Commission on Religion and Race, and stated clerk of the UPCUSA, Blake helped the ecumenical movement and the Presbyterian Church to make front-page news in the struggle for racial justice on numerous occasions. For northern-stream Presbyterians, Eugene Carson Blake epitomized the denomination's public witness for racial justice in church and society.

As "reunited" Presbyterians, however, we know less about the "team" of strategists and tacticians without whom Blake's public leadership would have faltered on issues of racial justice. African American staffers and lay leaders who were neither part of Blake's circle of direct reports nor among his intimate friends, but who carried the waters of baptism through which white and black Presbyterians passed to overcome their fatigue and discouragement, deserve to have their stories told as we reunited Presbyterians piece together a renewed vision of our denomination's commitment to racial justice and Christian unity. People like Edler Hawkins, Thelma Adair, Bryant George, Gladys Cole, Gayraud Wilmore, Mary Jane Patterson, J. Metz Rollins, Evelyn Gordon, and others have not yet received enough credit and gratitude for their parts in marshaling denominational and ecumenical resources for campaigns in Southern cities, such as Hattiesburg, Mississippi, during the years leading up to the historic passage of the Voting Rights Act (1963–65). Their ties to the wider African American community and the black freedom movement provided both the intelligence and the programmatic know-how on which Gene Blake and others relied to direct the denomination's course of action in the struggle for racial justice.

Let Justice Roll Down like Waters

On July 2, 1964, the most important civil rights legislation since Reconstruction (1875), Public Law 88–352, was passed by the United States Congress. The Civil Rights Act prohibited discrimination in public accommodations and in employment. Within weeks, the ravages of urban riots rocked the nation's cities beginning in Harlem, New York. Outbreaks in Brooklyn and Rochester, New York; Jersey City, New Jersey; Chicago, Illinois; and Philadelphia, Pennsylvania, resulted in millions of dollars in property losses. Six months later, on February 21, 1965, Malcolm X was assassinated in New York City.[14]

On May 26, 1965, the United States Congress passed a new voting rights bill, extending the provisions of the Twenty-fourth Amendment to the Constitution, which had been adopted a year earlier. While delivering his commencement speech at Howard University on June 4, 1965, President Lyndon Baines Johnson invoked the motto of the civil rights movement, "We Shall Overcome," to signal his earnest commitment to move ahead deliberately with a national agenda to incorporate African Americans into the mainstream of American life. Two months later, in August, the Watts section of Los Angeles was turned into a domestic war zone, when National Guard troops were called in to quell what was, at the time, the most devastating racial uprising in American history. Within eleven days, thirty-four people were killed, an estimated nine hundred injured, and more than thirty-five hundred arrested, and property damages was estimated at nearly $225 million.[15]

Gayraud Wilmore, social ethicist, historian, and considered by many the "dean emeritus" of black Presbyterianism, remembers the impact of these events on white and black Presbyterians. An unpublished account from his time as the executive director of the United Presbyterian Church Commission on Religion and Race (CORAR) is a vivid example of the extent to which Presbyterians were involved in aspects of the black freedom movement in America. Wilmore writes:

> After 1964 most of our activity was in the North. My two most vivid recollections are not of walking picket lines around the Forrest County Courthouse in Hattiesburg, but of helping Black Presbyterian church members barricade a street near their church during the violent uprising in Watts, and [on another occasion] calling my office in Manhattan from an exposed telephone booth while caught in a crossfire of bullets being traded by rioters and the police at a housing project in Newark, New Jersey. Many actions like these found the churches front and center through their professional staffs, but probably the only people who paid any attention at the time were F.B.I. agents, for one looks in vain for any accurate record of such church interventions in the secular literature dealing with the long hot summers of '64 to '68.[16]

If Wilmore is correct in his judgment that the more activist forms of interventions by the churches have been treated less than seriously in the secular literature, we must ask: Why? Was it that the *terms* for dealing with racial issues had changed so drastically by the mid-1960s that the secular literature could not grasp, much less understand, corresponding changes taking place in the public witness of the churches? Were the motives of churches such as ours, which stayed the course in the struggle for racial justice, obscured from public view or overshadowed by the anxious responses of the more evangelical and conservative churches?

Perhaps there was so little secular interest in the churches' internal debates over their role in public life because of cultural attitudes and interpretations of the "separation between church and state." Or could it simply (and sadly) be that the nation was not sufficiently convinced by the cause of disenfranchised African Americans to deliver on its promises of freedom and equality, to exercise its "religious" values in asserting the sanctity of all human life, and to strike down years of blatantly racist laws? While there are no easy answers to such questions or to the issues they represent, raising them helps us not only reflect on our past but also navigate our way through the rough waters we are bound to encounter as we embrace our theological and cultural diversity as God's gift, rather than as a social problem to solve or overcome. Looking back as Presbyterians, some of our most inviolable convictions about the church's mission to advance God's reign of justice in church and society have been honed in the midst of conflict, while working for the realization of our nation's highest values and democratic principles of freedom and liberty. We need only trace our lineage as a denomination back to John Calvin and Geneva to find ample evidence that, from its beginning, Reformed Christianity was intended to play an active role in public life.[17]

Bound Together in Christ's Name

Efforts in 1963 and 1964 to solidify cooperation between black and white Presbyterians met success in the founding of the Presbyterian Interracial Council (PIC). According to Wilmore, PIC's influence and effectiveness as an interracial "caucus" was strongest during the period immediately preceding the explosion of black identity programs and racial-ethnic organizations in the church (1966–1968).[18] By the mid-1960s the racial divide that separated whites and blacks had become the center of national attention. Mainline Protestant ecumenism, which supported strategies of racial integration embraced by liberal and more progressive Presbyterians, found itself unprepared for the dramatic shift taking place in the black freedom movement. "Black Power!" became the rallying cry of a new and more militant movement led by student activists in 1966. Racism was denounced as the personal and systematic expression of "white power." The tension between blacks and whites in the church intensified over the terms of interracial discourse, the goals of social activism, and the commitments to racial justice. Irreconcilable differences among conservative, liberal, and more radical Presbyterians finally came to a head in 1971 over mission strategies and the discretionary powers of programmatic agencies of the General Assembly to allocate denominational resources to the Angela Davis Defense Fund.

In the intervening years, between 1966 and 1971, Presbyterian churches were swept up in the most cataclysmic cycle of social change since Reconstruction, while also preparing the way for a new contemporary confession of faith. But by 1967, everything was up for grabs. The common cause of whites and blacks in the integrationist movement all but fell apart as the rising tide of demands for justice and equality reverberated through church and society.

A convergence of events toward the end of the 1960s signaled the start of a new chapter in interracial relations for white and black Presbyterians. Three events may be considered defining moments in what was to become a parting of the ways between black and white Presbyterians in the struggle for racial justice. These were the church's adoption of the Confession of 1967 (C '67), the church's reaction to the Black Manifesto, and the church's response to controversial decision of the Commission on Religion and Race (CORAR) to support the Angela Davis Defense Fund.

C '67, the last confessional statement adopted by Northern-stream Presbyterians prior to reunion in 1983, was the result of a 1956 overture intended either to revise the historic Westminster Shorter Catechism or to produce a contemporary brief statement of faith for the impending union in 1958 of the Presbyterian Church in the U.S.A. (PCUSA) and the United Presbyterian Church in North America (UPCNA). The new confession, which was to reflect and respond to contemporary life issues such as the role of science in religious faith, pluralism, diversity and inclusivity, and the equality of women, took four committees and almost ten years before a final version was adopted by the presbyteries.[19]

C '67 broke important new ground in terms of how God's gift of racial and ethnic particularity, expressed in human history and social location, is related to the church's mission of apostolicity in the world. By setting a theological mandate for the pursuit of racial justice before the churches, C '67 established a confessional basis for Presbyterian involvement in the struggle for racial justice. It (1) emphasized the ministry and message of Jesus Christ as incarnational or contextual theology and a model for doing ministry, in response to both "the human, social location of the biblical writings and the influence of our own history and culture"; (2) stressed the inherent value of addressing the growing alienation between Americans of European and African descent over matters of race in church and society, not only as a social issue but as a matter of justice about which God is concerned; and (3) boldly asserted that

> God has created the peoples of the earth to be one universal family. In his reconciling love, he overcomes barriers between brothers and breaks down every form of discrimination based on racial or ethnic difference, real or imaginary. . . . Therefore, the church labors for the abolition of all racial discrimination and ministers to those injured by it.[20]

With racial justice and racial reconciliation unequivocally affirmed in the scriptures and the confessions of the church as the mission of every Christian and world citizen, the landscape of interracial discourse among Presbyterians was irrevocably altered.

Through Times of Challenge, Controversy, and Hope

The fact that black and white Presbyterians shared (1) a common confessional tradition of Reformed faith, (2) a common commitment to the unity of Christ's body, and (3) a common passion for God's justice and for the nation's highest democratic ideals did not mean that they would easily overcome the equally strong racial and cultural identity issues that divided them. Furthermore, Black Power and the Black Theology movement had heightened a sense of militant racial consciousness among many black Presbyterians and underscored the need for powerful black caucus within the church. In response, Black Presbyterians United (BPU) was organized in 1968.[21] The caucus movement provided blacks in leadership and at the grass roots with a collective voice to participate in denominational decision making and with greater access to the resources needed to support the church's racial justice mission. With BPU established as a leading force in denominational affairs related to racial justice, the black Presbyterian presence was solidified by the time the Black Manifesto and the dispute over the Angela Davis defense fund reached their respective crisis proportions in the wider church.

Reeling from the Black Manifesto[22] and its call for "reparations," Presbyterians in North and South reacted similarly, by actions of their respective 1970 General Assemblies to reject the idea that white religious communities owed African Americans monetary compensation for their part as supporters of racism. And while both streams of the church refused to accept fully either the terms or the "penalties" of the changing interracial discourse as outlined in the Manifesto, each church body responded in tangible ways to the challenge that racism be dealt with theologically as a church-dividing issue among Presbyterians. The UPCUSA Program for the Self-Development of

People was one example of the church's positive response to the urgent matters at hand. From that point on, black and white Presbyterians worked together to support the self-development of groups affected by white racism and separately, in racial-ethnic caucuses, committed to keeping racial justice before the church as a priority item on its agenda.[23]

In many church circles, the details of the 1970s Angela Davis case have long been forgotten. What is remembered is the furor that erupted when it became public knowledge that the Council on Church and Race (COCAR) had allocated $10,000 from the denomination's Emergency Fund for Legal Aid to the Angela Davis defense fund. COCAR had been given the mandate by the General Assembly to act on its behalf in matters related to civil rights and racial justice issues. Months before the 183rd General Assembly began its meeting in Rochester, New York, in May 1971, the COCAR staff, their parent organization, and their coalition of supporters were already being tried and convicted by other Presbyterians over serious allegations that the Emergency Fund for Legal Aid had been misappropriated to benefit a young African American woman and university professor named Angela Davis. The reason given for the display of outrage across the church was that Davis, affiliated with the Communist Party in the United States, had been charged with supplying the guns that were used in a 1970 shoot-out in a San Raphael, California, courtroom, in which the judge and three others were killed.[24]

Much has been made of the Angela Davis case, and by all accounts it represented a crisis in the life of the United Presbyterian Church. Those who supported the action of COCAR seemingly did so out of a sense of faithfulness to a vision of the church as a household of freedom[25] and hospitality, a place of refuge, and an arbiter of justice in a world that systematically oppresses, wrongly incarcerates, and abandons those who have been most abused by America's system of justice. Those who objected to the action of COCAR seemingly did so also out of a sense of faithfulness to a vision of the church, but a very different vision from that of COCAR. Angela Davis and what her case represented became a lightning rod for clashing visions within the church over the mandate of the Council on Church and Race and over how far the United Presbyterian Church should extend itself and its resources to fulfill its commitments to racial justice.

The Angela Davis case seemingly pushed the envelope of the church's commitment to civil rights and racial justice almost beyond the reach of a vocal majority of Presbyterians. But how the Assembly resolved the matter raised hackles in the COCAR camp. To its credit, the Assembly stood by the mandate it had entrusted to the Council on Church and Race, rather than reverse itself under duress from the grass roots in the churches. COCAR was not dismantled, as many had wished and insisted should happen. Instead, the Assembly sent a message to COCAR expressing its "serious concern" over its decision in the Angela Davis case. In response, within weeks of the Assembly, and still outraged by the public embarrassment experienced by COCAR staff, a group of twenty African American Presbyterians raised $10,000 from their personal funds to demonstrate their conviction that the contribution to the Angela Davis defense fund had been the right and just thing to do, even if the whole church would not support the action taken on its behalf. Although nearly thirty years have passed, and though the details have faded from memory for many, the mere mention of the Angela Davis case still draws the kind of lively debate that leads me to believe that as white and black Presbyterians committed to Christian unity and racial justice, we still have a very long way to go.

The church of Jesus Christ is called in every age to proclaim the good news and to redress the particular manifestations of evil that stand in the way of the coming reign of God. Through faithful service, churches such as ours are to be (1) incarnations of Jesus Christ's ministry of *shalom*, (2) participants in shaping the public life of the nation according to its highest ideals, and (3) activists in the public witness against any form of injustice present inside or outside our gates. This is what it means to be adherents of the Reformed faith.

Our witness as black and white Presbyterians committed to Christian unity and racial justice has been honed through times of challenge, controversy, and hope. I suspect we will continue to struggle with issues of justice and reconciliation long into the new millennium. As a reforming people of faith, we are called to struggle for justice out of an abiding hope that along the way we are moving closer to becoming the new creation for which Jesus Christ prayed; that the world may believe, by our example, in the one whose name and mission we represent. May our struggles be blessed with the grace and love of God, and in their outcome, God's will be done!

NOTES

1. The title for this essay comes from the statement "A Call to Covenant Community" by the Covenant Network of Presbyterians. See the *Covenant Connection* newsletter 1, no. 5 (December 1998); and the Appendix in this volume.
2. The term *direct action* became synonymous with actions of nonviolent civil disobedience early in the struggle for African American civil rights. See Cheryl Lynn Greenberg, ed., *A Circle of Trust: Remembering SNCC* (New Brunswick, N.J.: Rutgers University Press, 1998), 39.
3. Cornel West, *Race Matters* (Boston. Beacon Press, 1993), 7.
4. See ibid., 3.
5. W. E. B. DuBois, *The Souls of Black Folk* (New York: Fawcett Publications, 1961), 23.
6. Nibs Stroupe and Inez Fleming, *While We Run This Race* (Maryknoll, N.Y.: Orbis Books, 1995), 3.
7. See R. Douglas Brackenridge, *Eugene Carson Blake: Prophet with Portfolio* (New York: Seabury Press, 1978), 91n.40, 204; Gayraud S. Wilmore, "Identity and Integration: Black Presbyterians and Their Allies in the Twentieth Century," in Milton J Coalter, John M. Mulder, and Louis B. Weeks, eds., *The Presbyterian Predicament: Six Perspectives* (Louisville, Ky.: Westminster/John Knox Press, 1990), 118; "Race and the Rights of Minorities in America," in *Social Policy Compilation* (Louisville, Ky.: Presbyterian Church (U.S.A.), 1991), chap. 8.
8. See Wilmore, "Identity and Integration," 110.
9. See Brackenridge, *Eugene Carson Blake,* 78.
10. Martin E. Marty, *Pilgrims in Their Own Land* (Boston: Little, Brown & Co., 1984), 154–64.
11. Brackenridge's biography is the source of information on Blake's church service.
12. See Brackenridge, *Eugene Carson Blake*, chap. 5, pp. 77ff.

13. See ibid., 89.
14. Alton Hornsby Jr., *Chronology of African-American History* (Detroit: Gale Research International, 1991), chap. 10.
15. See ibid.
16. From an unpublished text titled, "The Churches and the Civil Rights Movement," presented by Gayraud S. Wilmore on April 14, 1999, in Chicago, Illinois, as part of a public event jointly sponsored by Fourth Presbyterian Church and McCormick Theological Seminary.
17. John Calvin, *Institutes of the Christian Religion*, ed. John T. McNeill (Philadelphia: Westminster Press, 1960), II, 15, pp. 189–92.
18. See Wilmore, "Identity and Integration," 124.
19. Jack Rogers, *Reading the Bible and the Confessions the Presbyterian Way* (Louisville, Ky.: Geneva Press, 1999), 24ff.
20. In the *Book of Confessions*, 9.44. See Rogers's discussion of contextual theology and race in the Confession of 1967 in ibid., 27, 28, and 80.
21. See Wilmore, "Identity and Integration," 126.
22. The Black Manifesto was first presented to the National Black Economic Development Conference in Detroit, Michigan, by James Forman in April 1969. In a move that shocked the white middle-class liberal Protestant church, Forman entered New York City's prestigious Riverside Church on Sunday morning, May 4, 1969, and without notice interrupted the service to present the demands of the Black Manifesto to the nation. Widely publicized from that moment, the Black Manifesto accused the American churches and the white religious establishment of perpetrating racial injustice and perpetuating racial oppression since slavery. It demanded that the white churches repent of their role in the miscarriage of justice by paying $500 million in reparations to the black churches. See *Black Theology: A Documentary History, 1966–1979*, ed. Gayraud S. Wilmore and James H. Cone. (Maryknoll, N.Y.: Orbis Books, 1979).
23. See Joel L. Alvis, "A Presbyterian Dilemma: Ecclesiastical and Social Racial Policy in the Twentieth Century Presbyterian Communion," in *The Diversity of Discipleship: Presbyterians and Twentieth-Century Christian Witness*, ed. Milton J Coalter, John M. Mulder, and Louis B. Weeks (Louisville, Ky.: Westminster/John Knox Press, 1991), 205.
24. The Angela Davis case is discussed in numerous articles and church publications. For a fuller discussion, see Wilmore's and Alvis's accounts in *The Diversity of Discipleship*.

25. *Household of freedom* is a metaphor for a liberationist understanding of authority in the church of Jesus Christ that is developed by feminist scholar Letty M. Russell in her book *Household of Freedom: Authority in Feminist Theology* (Philadelphia: Westminster Press, 1987). In the chapter titled "Paradigms of Authority" (36), Russell draws on Martin Luther King Jr.'s vision of God's "world house" to illustrate what a community of partnership looks like in new creation. In the new creation that the church represents, no one is an outsider, not even an African American woman who happens to be a member of the Communist Party of the United States!

Of Quarks and Quirks

Colossians 1:15–20

Linda C. Loving

There are people who sometimes just burst into song—they can't help themselves. Some momentous occasion, some flash of insight, some joy or inspiration, and suddenly, words take flight in notes, as effortlessly as if life were an opera or a Rodgers and Hammerstein musical.

I can't help but think that is what happens in the first chapter of the letter to Colossians. The writer just gets so carried away with the revelation and joy of who Jesus is that he breaks into this extraordinary hymn, which was no doubt familiar to him and which becomes known to us as we read verses 15–20.

There is an ethereal and profound beauty to the words of this ancient hymn, which describe Christ as the ultimate meaning for which everything exists, has existed, will exist. New Testament scholar Eduard Schweizer observes, "Only the person who really knows of the world in its unreconciled and restless state, can properly sing of the one who contains everything. . . . Some of this 'foolish' joy comes alive in worship in the Gregorian chants, and in the wild melodies of African churches, but also in the songs of praise on the death of strict Jews in the Warsaw Ghetto, and in the persecuted Huguenots' psalms of praise. Like a strong secure tenor voice in a choir, the voice of the one who sings in this hymn will carry its hearers and readers along with it."[1]

We need to be carried by such a voice these days. We need this hymn from Colossians, so that we, too, know how to break into song as we are daily confronted with the unreconciled and restless state of the church and the world. The first half of the hymn extols Christ's role in creation: "the firstborn of all creation; for in him all things in heaven and on earth were created."

The second half of the hymn praises the reconciling nature of Christ: "through him God was pleased to reconcile to himself all things." In the center of the hymn, verse 17, are the words that provide the linchpin to this passage, and the linchpin to our understanding of Christ, of ourselves, of the church throughout the ages: "He himself is before all things, and in him all things hold together."

Christ is before all things. In other words, there is nothing we can cook up that Christ has not preceded, that Christ has not already known. He is before all things. He is before our councils, our doctrines, our soapboxes, our Books of Order; he is before our confessions, our denominations, our votes, our victories and defeats, our rules and regulations, our manuscripts, and our e-mails. Christ is before all things. He came first (just as he should continue to come first in all our lives). All the institutional ways we have of being the church, all our feeble attempts to embody the Christ, have come later. He is before all things.

"He himself is before all things, and in him all things hold together." In other words, just because he came first doesn't mean he's done. In him all things hold together—even to this day and in all the days to come. A kind of cosmic super glue across time. The power of Christ to bind us together is worth singing about, for we are accustomed to being fractured, fragmented, frustrated by differences, defensiveness, and discord.

"In him all things hold together." This is a vast promise spanning centuries and solar systems. At the same time, I believe this truth serves as a kind of molecular base for our individual spirits as well. This binding of Christ is at once as close as our next heartbeat and as distant as the farthest star. In him, all things, *all things*, hold together.

Kathleen Norris, in her book *Amazing Grace,* uses the example of the quark in describing the Trinity: "I love to read about quarks, those subatomic particles that exist in threes. There is no such thing as one quark, but only three interdependent beings; I picture them dancing together at the heart of things, part of the atomic glue that holds this world together, and to the atomic scientist at least, makes all things on earth more alike than different."[2] He is before all things, and in him all things hold together (making all things on earth more alike than different).

Perhaps it is time to put our spiritual quarks under the microscope. The Christ, dancing at the heart of all things since the beginning of time, holding all things together, makes all things on earth more alike than different. Then we come along, so busily and self-righteously defining all the things that make us more different that alike. Christians have given their lives, literally and figuratively, over the years for the sake of protecting the "truth" of their denomination or cause or identity. Spiritual quarks have been transformed into silly quirks—"No, our church does it *this* way"; "No, you would not be welcome at our communion table"; "We think you can be saved only if . . ." (fill in the blank according to (*a*) denominational guidelines, (*b*) personal preference, (*c*) marginalized group of the day, (*d*) none of the above).

Quarks into quirks. Then, by the grace of God, some of the quirks get translated back into quarks, when people and institutions let go of differences and agendas and allow for the truth of the Christ who "is before all things, and in him all things hold together," making all things on earth more alike than different.

Of course, talking about the things that make us alike seems far less interesting and attention-getting than talking about the things that seem to set us apart. Whispered comments in the narthex, at the potlucks, in the hallways of presbytery or General Assembly meetings don't often celebrate our unity in Christ, do they?

The good gossip is much more likely to be about the quirks of individuals—the things that seem peculiar and set apart, whether related to the individual's politics, sexuality, style of dress, or doctrine. No great biblical hymns, however, have been written about the quirks; rather, the hymns tell us of the unity of the Lord of all life.

If Christ holds all things together, we as Presbyterians and as Christians might well accept that Christ holds all people together, regardless of their religious orientation, or any other kind of orientation for that matter. Christ is before all things, and in him all things hold together.

Christ leads his disciples to experience the spiritual quarks that teach and offer unity across religion, class, race, nation, or any of the other categories that tend to emphasize differences. And so it is that Presbyterians have valued ecumenism from the very first days.

The great Buddhist leader Thich Nhat Hanh writes about our need to understand one another's traditions. When I read his words, I think not just about religious differences but about the many other creative differences that shape and define us—which are gifts of God and glued together by the Christ.

Hanh says that "sometimes it is more difficult to have a dialogue with people in our own tradition than with those of another tradition. Most of us have suffered from feeling misunderstood or even betrayed by those of our own tradition. But if brothers and sisters in the same tradition cannot understand and communicate with each other, how can they communicate with those outside their tradition? For dialogue to be fruitful, we need to live deeply our own tradition and, at the same time, listen deeply to others."[3]

Living deeply our own tradition and listening deeply to others—is that a lifestyle we might strive for in order to relinquish our obsession with one another's quirks? in order to discover what it really means to be bound together in Christ? Living deeply our own tradition and listening deeply to others, not just in terms of religious traditions but in terms of all the other kinds of traditions, expectations, experiences that shape us. Only in moving through the differences, even loving them, can we get to the place where we can glimpse the unity described in the hymn in Colossians.

While in Calcutta, Thomas Merton is said to have remarked,

"We are all one already! But we forget. We imagine that we are not. What we have to recover is our original unity. What we have to be is what we already are."[4]

In the book *Keepers of the Story*, Tony Cowan shares a story:

> Once upon a time . . . there was a young woman who longed to see God. . . . Stella was a simple girl who prayed and prayed and worked very hard . . . but she reached the age of sixteen, still not satisfied that she had seen God. So one day, she went to visit a wise old man who lived all alone out on the prairie . . . and said, "For as long as I can remember, I've had a burning desire to see God: not only to see God, but to look right into the pupil of his eye! If I could just do this I would be so happy. Can you tell me what I need to do so that this can happen?"
>
> The old man [said], "You must begin counting the stars at night. You must begin with the middle star in Orion's belt and start counting toward the east. You must take great care not to count any star twice, and you must not fail in your determination. When you have counted the ten thousandth star, you will be looking into the very light of God's eye."
>
> And so, Stella went out. That night, there was a new moon and there were very few clouds, so she was able to count the stars easily. . . . [S]he continued resolutely, night after night, week after week, month after month, always taking care to keep count and not get distracted. . . .
>
> What Stella didn't realize was that as she counted far into the eastern sky, the stars were revolving and turning through the heavens. And so, twelve months later, as she was approaching the ten thousandth star, she began to get the feeling that the pattern in the sky looked strangely familiar. . . . And as she counted the ten thousandth star, she suddenly realized that the ten thousandth star was the middle star in Orion's belt, the very star she had begun with twelve months before!
>
> Her eyes were dazzled with starlight and her mind and heart were filled instantly with the greatest joy and astonishment. Time seemed to stand still as she stood rapt in wonder, gazing at the ten thousandth star, and the star seemed to be gazing back at Stella with equal intensity. . . . She ran

through the night across the prairie to the house of the ancient wise man. . . .

"Judging from your radiant smile," said the old man, "you've counted the ten thousandth star tonight, and you have looked into the very eye of God. Yes?"

"Yes! Yes!" cried Stella . . . "the strangest thing happened. It turned out the ten thousandth star was somehow the very same star I had begun with, the middle star in Orion's belt. What can this mean?"

The old man smiled with delight. "It's simple," he murmured. "You begin by looking into the light of God's eyes, desperately desiring to see the light of God's eye. God was there all along. You just didn't realize it. The whole sky had to move through one complete revolution just so you could recognize what was right in front of you to start with! God moved heaven and earth to get you to this moment."[5]

To understand that in Christ all things hold together is such a moment. If we live deeply our own tradition and listen deeply to others; if we, as did Stella, allow ourselves the joy and astonishment of knowing that God would move heaven and earth to get us to the moment of understanding; if we, by grace, recover our original unity—then we, too, can break into ancient song. We can encounter the Christ and sense how we are indeed bound together in ways that make us more the same than different. And we can at last relinquish our obsession with the quirks of humankind and live reflecting the image of the one in whom all things, *all things*, hold together.

NOTES

1. Eduard Schweizer, *The Letter to the Colossians* (Minneapolis: Augsburg Publishing House, 1982), 87.
2. Kathleen Norris, *Amazing Grace* (New York: Riverhead Books, 1998), 290.
3. Thich Nhat Hanh, *Living Buddha, Living Christ* (New York: Riverhead Books, 1995), 7.
4. Quoted in Megan McKenna and Tony Cowan, *Keepers of the Story* (Maryknoll, N.Y.: Orbis Books, 1997), 20.
5. Ibid., 12–13.

Multiculturalism or Cultural Circumcision?

Acts 10; 11:18

Karen Hernández-Granzen

As I was writing this sermon, I was struck by how apropos it is that I also am preparing to give birth to our second multiracial and multicultural child. Giving birth to this sermon has been very labor intensive, because I am fully aware of the challenge of addressing two audiences—white people and people of color, who have similar as well as different issues—and because my own battle with internalized oppression continues to have a paralyzing, debilitating effort on my ability to use my God-given voice. For the sake of our children's full acceptance and participation in the life of the church, however, and in preparation for ministry in the third millennium, I have tried to rely on the power and inspiration of Holy Spirit to deliver a message that I hope will encourage others who are considering multiracial and multicultural ministry to say, "Heme aquí Señor, envíame a mí"—"Here am I [Lord]; send me!" (Isa. 6:8).

I begin with words from the president's State of the Union address in February 1997, words also printed in Westminster Presbyterian Church of Trenton's one hundredth anniversary book in 1998, since they apply not only to the United States of America but also to the Presbyterian Church (U.S.A.):

> Our diversity is not our weakness, it is our strength. . . . [W]e
> do not share a common past, but we can share a common
> future.

C. S. Lewis, in his book *The Great Divorce,* described a vision
of hell as a place where people move continually away from one
another because they just cannot get along with each other. They
choose instead to abandon their houses and entire blocks and
neighborhoods and to build new houses at the periphery of hell,
thereby creating an ever-expanding vacant center, with houses at
the periphery and with the center abandoned behind them.[1]
Joseph Barndt says that Lewis's description of hell could actually
be a "description of white flight from the city after WW II and
the emergence of suburbs in the United States" (and today's
exurbs). He goes on to say that with suburbs came the demand
for transportation systems to separate suburban whites from
people of color in the inner cities. When I lived in Los Angeles,
I drove the multilane and multilevel system ironically called
"freeways." These have contributed to suburbanites' experienc-
ing feelings of isolation and have even led some to minimize the
effects of the commute by turning to alcohol and tranquilizers.[2]

Barndt's excellent book *Dismantling Racism: The Continuing
Challenge to White America* is helpful for our meditation on
multiculturalism in the church, because you can't talk about
multiculturalism without first talking about racism, and in order
to truly engage in introspection and dialogue, it is essential to use
language that doesn't attack or produce guilt. Barndt analyzes
the dehumanizing effects racism has on all of us—"people of
color and white people alike—indoctrinated and socialized in
such a way as to be made into 'prisoners of racism.' " He notes
that every antiracist leader, from Frederick Douglas to Martin
Luther King Jr., emphasized how both white people and people
of color are debilitated by racism, and that the goal is liberation
for all people.[3]

Barndt utilizes creative and disturbing images to resensitize
white Americans who have become anesthetized to the pain of
living in a prison. He writes that "white people, too, live in a
'racial ghetto.' Although we may have built the walls ourselves,

the resulting isolation and its effects are equally harmful. We live in a ghetto, on a reservation, in a separated, cut-off state of existence. We are racially, institutionally, and culturally segregated from people who are not white. Our communities are sterile, homogenous places of look-alike, dress-alike, act-alike conformity."[4]

People of color also anesthetize themselves from the pain of racism. Hyun K. Chung's description of Asian women's experience is also descriptive of what many other people of color experience. Asian women have defended themselves from the constant and sustained experiences of "shame, guilt, and self-hate by numbing themselves, thus creating a pseudo-safety of non-feeling." This behavior is dysfunctional because the oppressed are stripped of their power to resist. This numbing process is called the "separation sin" because it causes persons to be "separated from themselves, each other, and the God of Life."[5]

Little did I know that, since my conception, the Holy Spirit had been preparing me for a multiracial and multicultural ministry. I am a multiracial, multicultural, and bilingual Newyorrican (a Puerto Rican born in New York) and, as such, native Taino, European Spaniard, and black African. I have been an urbanite practically all my life, having lived in New York City, Los Angeles, San Francisco, Chicago, and Trenton. I have witnessed to my dismay how the suburbs have helped perpetuate so-called separate-but-equal worshiping communities of suburban whites and people of color in the inner cities. Many remnant white congregations that have remained in the city also have maintained so-called separate-but-equal relationships with neighborhood churches that are comprised of people of color. I find it very disturbing that many Christians, whites and people of color alike, are not convicted by the fact that Sunday morning continues to be the most segregated time in our society, and the church the most segregated institution.

Barndt's image of hell comes to mind when I think of mainline urban European American churches who have not enthusiastically welcomed the "mission at their doorstep" opportunity when their neighborhood's racial-ethnic demographic composition changed. Instead, many respond to declining church membership due to "white flight" by fleeing to the suburbs, abandoning church buildings, and leaving behind God's beloved communities.

A thesis project written by my husband, Michael Granzen, provides substantial evidence of the "conspiracy of silence" that exists in the church in regard to open and sincere discussion of issues about race.[6] Robert Terry, an analyst and educator on racism and racial justice, puts it succinctly: "To be white in America is not to have to think about it,"[7] and I would add, not to have to talk about it. Barndt asserts that European American congregations (unfortunately, Presbyterian churches included) have become complacent and comfortable in their "white ghetto-ized churches in white ghettoized neighborhoods," no longer questioning whether this situation is a scandal to the gospel.[8]

The *Book of Order* contains strong "shall" statements on inclusiveness. Our constitution states that "the congregation *shall* welcome all persons who respond in trust and obedience to God's grace in Jesus Christ. . . . No person shall be denied membership because of race, ethnic origin, worldly condition, or any other reason not related to profession of faith. Each member must seek the grace of openness in extending the fellowship of Christ to all persons. . . . Failure to do so constitutes a rejection of Christ himself and causes a scandal to the gospel" (G-5.0103).[9] Yet, instead of being scandalized by how some racially exclusive churches contradict our witness to the Lord's gift of unity, the tendency is to rationalize the existence of these churches by stating, "This is just human nature," or by quoting church growth experts who claim that homogeneous communities are the most effective strategy for optimal church growth, or by clinging to the notion that being a good steward of God's resources means investing primarily in new church developments and redevelopments that are racially specific because their growth probability is much greater and the church is guaranteed a greater return per dollar.

When I attended a Presbyterian Health, Education and Welfare Association antiracism leadership-training event led by Joseph Barndt and the team from Crossroads Ministry, I almost jumped out of my seat to affirm publicly how his interpretation of Peter and Cornelius's *cara a cara* (face to face) encounter in Acts 10 and the reaction of the circumcised believers described in chapter 11 resonated with my own interpretation. Just as some "circumcised believers" thought that God-fearing Gentiles must first become culturally and religiously Jews, some European American Christians have explicitly or implicitly expected Native Americans, African Americans, Hispanic Americans, and Asian Americans to leave their cultures at the door of the sanctuary as they enter a Eurocentric-style worship service and thereby to experience "cultural circumcision."

Culture has a dictatorial power that influences our thoughts and behavior by creating unconscious, built-in blinders that become hidden and unspoken assumptions.[10] For instance, there is a hidden and unstated assumption prevalent in the dominant culture of the United States, and that is that "white/Anglo" is not an ethnic group. Minority cultural groups are called ethnics, thereby implying that they are different from the norm because of their race and culture, the norm being the culture of the white/Anglo. Church historian and theologian Catherine González, in "The Diversity with Which We Begin," states that this unspoken assumption denies the fact that the white/Anglo worship style is influenced and controlled by their culture. Denying this reality prevents "the unraveling of cultural processes," and thus the white/Anglo worship style becomes superior and the norm.[11] The emphatic declaration "This is not Presbyterian!" made by many Presbyterians, white and people of color alike, is more often than not a reference to some element of worship that is not Eurocentric. The other hidden and unspoken assumption is that minority cultures have a uniformity that doesn't actually exist. For instance, the term *Hispanic American* denies the differences that exist among Hispanics from the Caribbean and Central and South America.[12]

Due to the complex, dictatorial power of culture, we all must desperately cling to the faith-knowledge that the Holy Spirit is continually transforming our conscious and unconscious conformity to the oppressive elements of this world by renewing our minds (Rom. 12:2). We can make a choice to personally engage in the renewing process of our minds by exposing ourselves to scripture. Justo González's "grammar for reading the Bible in Spanish" suggests we read scripture in the vocative voice: "The purpose of scripture is not so much to interpret it as to allow it to interpret us and our situation."[13] We've been meditating on tough issues of race and culture that describe our present reality; now let us focus once again on scripture to help us gain insights about ourselves and our context.

The title "The Acts of the Apostles" is truly a misnomer, because the body of Jesus Christ cannot accomplish its mission without the power of the Holy Spirit. Since the church's inception at Pentecost, the Holy Spirit revealed that the church of Jesus Christ would be "multilingual and multicultural, [since] at Pentecost God sanctioned linguistic and cultural pluralism."[14] Based on this interpretation, "Babel was a monument to the arrogance of one people; Pentecost on the other hand should lead to the humiliation of anyone who thinks their language is superior to others."[15]

As recorded in the Gospels, Jesus set the stage for the type of church the Holy Spirit would empower by personally incarnating a ministry to the unwelcome strangers, the inferior untouchables of his society. Luke 4 illustrates how Jesus, even at the risk of losing his own life, revealed God's clear preference for the poor, the captives, the blind, the oppressed, and even for the ritually unclean and culturally different Gentiles.

The Holy Spirit orchestrated the process needed to transform Peter's mind about the Gentile people and his exclusive understanding of the mission of the church. For us to truly grasp why a transforming process was indispensable, we need to be reminded of how Peter's religious training and cultural conditioning influenced his perception of Gentiles. Anticipating Peter's understandable reluctance, the Holy Spirit commanded Peter to go with Cornelius's men because, as Peter said so tactlessly upon entering Cornelius's home, "it is unlawful for a Jew to associate with or to visit a Gentile" (Acts 10:28). Most law-abiding Jews such as Peter would avoid even more any contact with a Roman centurion, since the Roman Empire encouraged their people to mix their religions.[16] Peter's next statement, "God has shown me that I should not call anyone profane and unclean," reveals his previous hidden opinion about Gentiles (Acts 10:28). The process began with a vision that was interpreted three times in order to make absolutely sure Peter understood; proceeded to an actual *cara a cara* encounter with God's children, which quickly gave him an opportunity to implement this new divine insight; and ended with the undeniable evidence of the Holy Spirit's presence and approval when the God-fearing Gentiles received the gift of the Holy Spirit, spoke in tongues, and worshiped God!

Through this process Peter, the great teacher of the gospel, actually became a learner: when he encounters Cornelius *cara a cara*, he declares with conviction: "I truly understand that God shows no partiality, but in every nation anyone who fears [God] and does what is right is acceptable to [God]" (Acts 10:34–35).

Not only white people but people of color in our church also need to experience a transforming and renewing of their minds in order to be freed from the debilitating effects of internalized oppression. Internalized oppression manifests itself in many ways, such as "system beating, blaming the system, anti-white avoidance of contact, denial of cultural heritage, and lack of understanding of the political significance of differences."[17]

Since our meditation focuses on multiculturalism, let me share the story of how a Hispanic Presbyterian church experienced liberation from denying their cultural heritage. Prior to my serving Iglesia Presbiteriana Betel in Los Angeles for six years as youth director, I had always worshipped and served Hispanocentric churches that not only incorporated the Spanish language but also incorporated Hispanic music and instruments and a "fiesta" (festive) worship style. My first experience of culture shock in the church occurred when I worshiped for the first time at Iglesia Betel. Even though worship was conducted in Spanish, every other element of worship was Eurocentric, including the sole use of organ music. Some Hispanic Presbyterian churches in Los Ranchos Presbytery had even accomplished their ultimate goal of creating a "Eurocentric," traditional worship service that was even better than that of some white congregations.

The transforming process at Iglesia Betel began with the pastor, the Reverend Héctor Delgado. Through the power of the Holy Spirit and the affirmation of the pastor's effectiveness in ministry at local, regional, and national levels, Héctor acquired the inner strength required to overcome what Paulo Freire calls "fear of freedom."[18] He became empowered to resist conforming to a prescribed Eurocentric style of worship and consequently accepted the risk of being rejected and ostracized by his peers and labeled a nonconformist. After two years, as our Hispanocentric worship style became more appealing to the Hispanics in our community, membership grew. We became the first Hispanic new church development to organize in the entire Synod of Southern California, fifty years after the last one was organized. Synod and presbytery events became opportunities to share our Hispanic culture, not in a humiliating, entertaining manner but as genuine expressions of worship done with integrity and sincerity. What I learned through this experience is that there is a direct correlation between my appreciation of my Hispanic heritage and the manner in which others will appreciate and experience it as well.

The Holy Spirit also orchestrated a process for law-abiding, circumcised Jews to stop insisting that God-fearing Gentiles become circumcised and obey the law of Moses. The council at Jerusalem created the environment to discuss the issues openly. Peter was invited to share what the Holy Spirit had revealed to him though his *cara a cara* encounter with Cornelius. All this led to the council's decision not to impose circumcision as a requirement for church membership but only to expect Gentiles to obey the essentials: "abstain only from things polluted by idols and from fornication and from whatever has been strangled and from blood" (Acts 15:1–29).

Notice how the church dealt with their challenging situation. They acknowledged the Holy Spirit's presence, created an environment for open discussion, came to a decision, and communicated that decision. Cultural circumcision of people of color will continue to make the churches dehumanizing if mainline Eurocentric churches do not genuinely address the complex issues.

It would be very naive and self-destructive for a predominantly white Presbyterian church that is considering redeveloping into a multiracial and multicultural congregation not to acknowledge the inherent obstacles. When I was installed as pastor of Westminster Church, Justo González's sermon vividly portrayed the challenge, but he also heralded the call:

> [W]hile the encounter with many peoples and cultures is intellectually and emotionally enriching, it is also painful, and many people feel justified to resent it. As the old certainties provided by more limited horizons are challenged by people coming out of different experiences, many respond in fear and bitterness. . . . [W]e must confess that we are all tempted to privilege our own people, our own tribe, our own language, our own nation.

I submit to you that this will be one of the most difficult aspects of Christian ministry in this country in the decades to come. It will be so difficult that many will be content with preaching and with believing a supposed gospel that does not challenge our exclusivisms and our tribalisms. And yet, faithfulness requires that we continually put forth the vision of John, of "'a great multitude that no one could count, from every nation, from all tribes and peoples and languages' [Rev. 7:9], whom God also loves."[19]

Realizing a God-given mission and vision to become multiracial and multicultural by moving from a Eurocentric to a multicultural style of worship requires the delicate embrace of contemporary and traditional styles of worship. Some members will feel the church is moving too fast, while others will feel the church isn't moving fast enough; therefore, open communication by "carefronting" (caring enough to confront in a constructive manner) is crucial.[20] The Holy Spirit is orchestrating the birthing process of Westminster Church's transformation into a multiracial and multicultural beloved community of God. We are witnessing the Holy Spirit's presence and affirmation when Euro-American members can no longer feel comfortable worshiping in an all-white, Eurocentric church, and when people of color overcome their internalized oppression and are empowered to share their diverse gifts of worship with integrity and sincerity.

Urban centers are not forever damned because of their multiracial and multicultural diversity; they are forever blessed! "And I saw the holy city, the new Jerusalem, coming down out of heaven from God, prepared as a bride and a bridegroom adorned for each other. And I heard a loud voice from the throne saying, 'See, the home of God is among mortals. God will dwell with them; they will be God's peoples' " (Rev. 21:2–3).[21] Multicultural ministry is challenging, but it can also be very enriching and transforming for white people and people of color. Cities provide the "sacred space" whereby, as John S. Dunne wrote, "cultures can know and touch each other as never before, persons can be aware as never before of what was from the beginning always real: their common humanity and the many manifestations of the one ultimate mystery."[22]

Over two hundred congregations within the Presbyterian Church (U.S.A.) already have said, "Heme aquí Señor, envíame a mí," to be a multiracial and multicultural community of God servers. They have been empowered by the Holy Spirit to overcome cultural barriers in order to experience more fully the mystery of God. Let us pray that during the third millennium, multicultural ministries will be not just a desperate answer to church growth but a passionate yearning to experience more fully the manifestation of the God of all nations, tribes, peoples, and cultures.

Amen.

NOTES

1. C. S. Lewis, *The Great Divorce* (New York: Macmillan Co., 1946), 18ff.

2. Joseph Barndt, *Dismantling Racism: The Continuing Challenge to White America* (Minneapolis: Augsburg, 1991), 54.

3. Ibid., 6–7.
4. Ibid., 110.
5. Hyun K. Chung, *Struggle to Be the Sun Again* (Maryknoll, N.Y.: Orbis Books, 1990), 41–42.
6. Michael A. Granzen, "Breaking through the Plate Glass Window: A Study on Race and Religion in Elizabeth, New Jersey" (thesis, Princeton Theological Seminary, 1998), 1ff.
7. Robert Terry, "The Negative Impact on White Values," in *Impacts of Racism on White Americans*, ed. Benjamin P. Bowser and Raymond Hunt (Newbury Park, Calif.: Sage Publications, 1981), 120.
8. Barndt, *Dismantling Racism*, 140.
9. *The Constitution of the Presbyterian Church* (U.S.A.) (Louisville, Ky.: Office of the General Assembly, 1998).
10. Edward T. Hall, *Beyond Culture* (New York: Doubleday & Co., Anchor Books, 1976), 220.
11. Catherine G. González, "The Diversity with Which We Begin," *Reformed Theology and Worship*, Spring 1987, 71.
12. Ibid.
13. Justo L. González, *Mañana: Christian Theology from a Hispanic Perspective* (Nashville: Abingdon Press, 1990), 86–86.
14. I. G. Malcolm, "The Christian Teacher in the Multicultural Classroom," *Journal of Christian Education* 74 (1982): 53.
15. Ibid.
16. Justo L. González, *Hechos*, Comentario bíblico hispanoamericano (Miami: Editorial Caribe, 1992), 176.
17. Valerie Batts, "Modern Racism: New Melody for the Same Old Tunes," *EDS Occasional Papers* (1998), 11.
18. Paulo Freire, *Pedagogy of the Oppressed* (New York: Continuum, 1970), 31.
19. Justo L. González, "A Tale of Two Scrolls" (sermon preached at the installation service of Karen Hernández-Granzen in Trenton, New Jersey, 1995).
20. David Augsburger, *Caring Enough to Confront: How to Understand and Express Your Feelings toward Others* (Scottdale, Pa.: Herald Press, 1980).
21. *The New Testament and Psalms: An Inclusive Version*, ed. Victor Roland Gold et al. (New York and Oxford: Oxford University Press, 1995), 408.
22. Paul F. Knitter, *No Other Name?* (Maryknoll, N.Y.: Orbis Books, 1992), 211.

Appendix

A Call to Covenant Community

As disciples of Jesus Christ and members of the Presbyterian Church (U.S.A.), in reliance on the promise of God's grace, we make the following affirmations about our faith and our church:

We affirm faith in Jesus Christ who proclaimed the reign of God by preaching good news to the poor, binding up the broken-hearted and calling all to repent and believe the good news. It is Christ whose life and ministry forms and disciplines all we say and do.

The church we seek to strengthen is built upon the hospitality of Jesus, who said, "Whoever comes to me I will not cast out." The good news of the gospel is that all—those who are near and those who were far off—are invited; all are members of the household and citizens of the realm of God. No one has a claim on this invitation and none of us becomes worthy, even by sincere effort to live according to God's will. Grateful for our own inclusion, we carry out the mission of the church to extend God's hospitality to a broken and fearful and lonely world.

The people of God are called to be "light to the nations." As God's people, we have a commission rather than a privilege. We believe that the place of the church is in the world and for the world: living the good news, proclaiming grace, working with others for justice, freedom and peace. This Christian faith has an inevitable public and political dimension. Because we believe that God is at work in culture

212

and community beyond the church, the church need not be afraid to look and listen for God's voice from outside its own sphere.

The words of scripture provide life and nourishment; as the psalmist says, they are desirable, delicious, sweet. The Bible is the evidence of God's long, patient and persistent relationship with communities and persons of faith. It is the one true, reliable witness to God's self-giving in Jesus Christ. The process of discerning God's Word in the words of scripture depends on the faithful reading of the Bible by those who seek the guidance of the Holy Spirit. We are committed to the ongoing task of finding in scripture God's call to live out the Christian life in our day and time. We embrace gifts of scholarship, research and dialogue as we seek to understand the Bible's relevance to the ever-changing needs of the world and to circumstances which scripture does not explicitly address.

We seek the gift of unity among all who confess the name of Jesus Christ as Lord. Unity is Christ's prayer for those who would follow him, "so that the world might believe." We hope to maintain communion fellowship with all whose lives are guided by the Christian creeds and by the confessions of Reformed faith. We pledge to strengthen our ties to those who are at risk of being excluded by recent legislative actions of our church. We also want to live in unity with those whose views are different from ours.

Because nothing in life or death can separate us from God's love, we pray that the issues before us will not separate us from one another.

Therefore we covenant together to:
Welcome, in the name of Christ, all whom God calls into community and leadership in God's church;
Reach out in solidarity and compassion to all who are wounded or excluded by recent legislative actions of our church;

Continue to be faithful to the Presbyterian Church (U.S.A.), supporting its mission in Christ's name to God's world;

Reaffirm our denomination's historic understanding that "God alone is Lord of the conscience" (G-1.0301) both for ourselves and for those with whom we disagree;

Trust sessions and presbyteries to ordain those called by God, through the voice of the church, who are "persons of strong faith, dedicated discipleship, and love of Jesus Christ as Savior and Lord" and whose "manner of life demonstrates the Christian gospel in the church and the world" (G-6.0106a);

Seek pastoral and theological solutions to divisions in the church;

Maintain dialogue, study, and prayer in the spirit of Christ with those with whom we differ, seeking to understand the deeper roots of our disagreements;

Seek God's will for the church through the presence of Christ, the study of scripture, the guidance of our historic confessions, and the dynamic work of the Holy Spirit;

Encourage officers and governing bodies of the church to join us in this covenant.

As we covenant together in Christ, we commit ourselves to encourage one another through prayer, counsel, and mutual support, through times of challenge, controversy, and hope.